Prescriptions for Success in Heterogeneous Classrooms

Prescriptions for Success
in
Heterogeneous Classrooms

by Sandra L. Schurr

nmsa ®

NATIONAL MIDDLE SCHOOL ASSOCIATION

Sandra L. Schurr is the Director of the National Resource Center for Middle Grades/High School Education at the University of South Florida. A veteran teacher and administrator, Dr. Schurr is widely known for her dynamic style and endless supply of imaginative activities. National Middle School Association is most grateful to her for corraling a good number of teaching strategies and casting them in this unique diagnosis/prescription format. Classroom teachers will thank her as well.

Appreciation is extended to Greg Jordan of the Resource Center for his work in preparing the initial manuscript and to Mary Mitchell for designing the publication and readying it for printing.

Finally, the many authors and publishers, portions of whose works are included in this volume, are gratefully recognized for granting permission to reproduce excerpts from their published sources.

COVER DESIGN BY MELANIE MADDUX

Copyright© 1995
National Middle School Association

PRINTED IN THE UNITED STATES OF AMERICA

ISBN 1-56090-097-0

To Andy, Ryan, and Matthew Schurr,

my grandsons and my legacies to a world that must learn to value diversity.

CONTENTS

FOREWORD

Although admittedly fraught with difficulty, the shift from homogeneous grouping to heterogeneous grouping certainly will continue to advance in middle level schools. While such a move may counter long-standing tradition, deeply engrained practices, and even apparent logic it should be recognized that ability grouping never has had any substantial support from research, while research in support of heterogeneous grouping accumulates. Middle level educators now readily acknowledge that the middle school concept calls for heterogeneous grouping. But while intellectually supporting this practice, classroom teachers understandably seek help in learning how to deal with the diversity of abilities, interests, and learning styles that comes with heterogeneity.

Prescriptions for Success in Heterogeneous Classrooms provides help in abundant measure. Here, in her inimitable style, Sandra Schurr sets forth 28 specific learning strategies. Each is cast as a *prescription* applicable for students whose *diagnosis* reveals certain conditions. The activities are fully detailed and illustrated. Reproducible pages accompany most of them. Contained in this publication, the reader will find a fascinating array of imaginative teaching techniques that will engage youngsters and get their creative juices flowing.

The distance between this handbook and the classroom is about as short as is possible. Teachers will see how practical these strategies are and will quickly recognize how they can and should be put to immediate use. Interdisciplinary teams will have a professional field day as they draw upon this resource during common planning time.

These activities are not merely more intriguing ways of "instructing," gimmicks to dress up teaching as telling. They are rather very much in concert with the ongoing shift in the teacher's role from being an instructor to becoming a director of learning, a creator of engaging activities through which students acquire knowledge and gain real understanding.

Prescriptions for Success in Heterogeneous Classrooms is a rich and ready resource for teachers who desire to be truly effective in dealing with the diversity that characterizes middle level classrooms.

— John H. Lounsbury

A MESSAGE FROM THE DOCTOR

This book of instructional strategies represents a collection of classroom activities that work extremely well with diverse groups of students at the middle level. All ideas have been field tested over and over again with teachers of many disciplines, with students of varied abilities, with parents of multiple cultures, and with curriculum supervisors of differing philosophies.

The strategies were selected from a larger number of tasks because they were:

1. central to core subject areas;
2. generic and applicable to an assortment of topics within major disciplines;
3. motivating to students;
4. manageable for teachers;
5. comprehensible to parents;
6. compatible with more authentic types of assessment; and
7. fun for the author to write.

The format is simple. Each strategy has a specific name or title attached to it with a corresponding "DIAGNOSIS" label that is intended to show teachers what types of student are most likely to benefit from the "PRESCRIPTION." The strategies also lend themselves to the continued *cognitive growth* and *mental health* of both heterogeneous groups of students and teams of teachers who value and celebrate the diverse cultures, interests, aptitudes, and ability levels represented by the early adolescent in today's schools.

As the reader begins to become acquainted with this book, it is suggested that time be spent first on reviewing all of the strategies for their relevance and appeal to a given group of students before personal decisions are made by the teacher on whether to try out an idea. This approach will demonstrate both the "scope" of the strategies and their "adaptability" to most teaching styles and course objectives.

The author sincerely hopes that these strategies will be "just what the doctor ordered" for your middle level classroom.

Be sure to refill as often as necessary!

Dr. Sandra Schurr

1. Generic Skill Cards for Reading a Short Story or Novel

Effective for students who:

- are each reading a different story or novel in class
- are reading the same story or novel in small groups
- are reading at varied instructional levels

 Create a set of general skill cards similar to the ones below. These skill cards are designed to infuse thinking skills into the language arts curriculum so that each student or group of students can be reading a variety of different books and yet still be able to discuss what they are reading with one another. Write your tasks out on large file cards that can be reproduced in sets. You might even want to color code the skill cards so that one color includes all of the character–related tasks while another color includes all of the vocabulary–related tasks or thinking skill–related tasks.

Character Description *1*

Select one of the main characters and find words, phrases, and short passages that describe him/her. Organize your descriptions into these categories using a chart format: physical appearance, behavior traits, personal feelings/attitudes, and personality quirks.

Character Analysis *3*

Select one of the main characters and show how he/she influences the actions and behaviors of other characters in the story. Do this through a series of cause and effect drawings.

Character Development *2*

Select one of the main characters and describe how he/she changes throughout the story. Create a timeline of significant events that bring about these changes.

Character Moods and Moments *4*

Select one of the main characters and describe a situation that made him/her experience each of the following emotions: anger, excitement, sadness, frustration, and puzzlement.

Conduct a Character Interview   *5*

Plan an ideal birthday party of one of the characters. What would he/she want to do, receive as gifts, invite as guests, and eat for food?

Character Comparisons   *6*

Compare and contrast important characters in the story to actual people you know. Describe their similarities and differences.

Who's Who   *7*

Create a series of "who's who" cards for each major and minor character in the book. Give their names, their roles in the story, and descriptions of things they do or actions they take.

Communicating Characters   *8*

Design a set of greeting cards, post cards, or calling cards that one character from the story might send or give to another.

Setting Overview   *9*

Answer the following questions about the theme and focus of the story:
• What is the story about?
• Where and when does the story take place?
• Who are the main characters in the story?
• Why is the setting important to the story?
• How does the author develop the plot in the story?

Changing the Setting   *10*

Write a brief summary telling how this story might be different if the action took place in a different historical period, in a different geographical location, or in a fantasy context.

Researching the Setting   *11*

Conduct additional research about the actual setting of the story and collect factual information about it that could be used by the author to rewrite portions of the story.

Reporting the Events   *12*

Assume you are a newspaper reporter and write a news or feature story about a key event from the story.

Acting Out   *13*

Choose a series of scenes from the story and act them out.

Creating Plot Visuals   *14*

Construct one of the following visuals to show the interrelationships of characters, events, and/or themes in the story: web, flow chart, Venn Diagram, or fishbone.

Thinking Skill: Fact vs. Opinion   *15*

Record ten facts and ten opinions directly from the story. Be able to defend your choices.

Thinking Skill: Predicting Outcomes *16*

Locate passages from various sections of the story that give you clues as to what is coming next. This technique is called "foreshadowing" and is popular with good authors and readers.

Thinking Skill: Drawing Conclusions *20*

Design a graph that plots the excitement or interest level of events from the story. Use an excitement/interest level range of 1–10 on the vertical axis and a brief description of specific story events on the horizontal axis.

Thinking Skill: Evaluating Outcomes *17*

Select any two characters from the story, any two settings from the story, or any two events from the story. Describe how they are alike and how they are different.

Word Choices *21*

Find special words, phrases, or sentences in the story that cater to the five senses of sight, sound, taste, touch, and smell. Write these out in an interesting "word collage" complete with appropriate graphics.

Thinking Skill: Evaluating Outcomes *18*

Generate a list of criteria for a good story and then use this list to draw conclusions about the quality of this one.

22. Words That Challenge *22*

Choose the ten most difficult, unusual, or expressive words from the story and write out their definitions as used in the context of the story.

Thinking Skill: Making Inferences *19*

Infer where the author might have gotten ideas for this story. Consider sources he/she might have used for characterization, setting, and plot.

Being Word Wise *23*

Compose a series of classified ads based on the story. Consider lost and found ads, help wanted ads, items for sale ads, real estate ads, and personal ads. Choose your words carefully!

Word Riddles *24*

Compose a series of simple riddles that describe characters, settings, and events from the story.

Refill as often as necessary

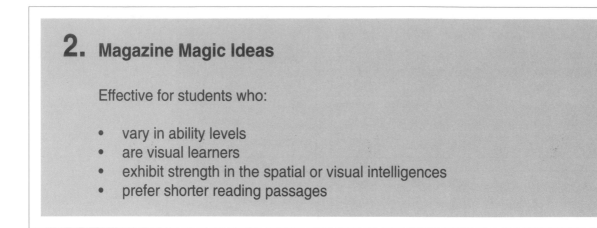

2. Magazine Magic Ideas

Effective for students who:

- vary in ability levels
- are visual learners
- exhibit strength in the spatial or visual intelligences
- prefer shorter reading passages

 These activities require the use of magazines as springboards for designing and completing a wide range of learning exercises in the basic skill areas.

1. Construct a magazine report. To do this, the student should:	a. Choose a topic to research. b. Collect 8 to 10 facts about the topic. c. Construct a booklet of 8 to 10 blank pages. d. Write out one fact on a separate page of the booklet. e. Cut out magazine pictures to illustrate each fact page. f. Add a cover and title page to the booklet.
2. Cut out a series of interesting and action-oriented illustrations from a variety of magazines.	Paste each illustration on a separate piece of paper and have students write out a set of statements expressing what he/she felt happened before the event depicted in the illustration and what might happen after or as a result of the event depicted in the illustration.
3. Collect a series of magazine illustrations around a central theme for any subject area such as careers, ecology, computers, superstars, or politics.	Use each of these illustrations as a set of springboards for directing students to write a series of factual statements or paragraphs presenting relevant information on the theme's content.

4. Ask students to browse through magazines, flyers, pamphlets, or even newspapers to locate pictures around a common topic of their choice.	Instruct students to cut out the pictures and paste them in collage fashion around the edge of a large sheet of paper. They are then to use the pictures as a basis for writing a set of special sentences relevant to the topic and that include the following sentence structures: a. an interrogative sentence b. an exclamatory sentence c. an imperative sentence d. a declarative sentence e. a compound sentence f. a complex sentence g. a sentence containing a direct quotation h. a sentence containing an indirect quotation i. a sentence containing words or phrases in a series separated by commas j. a sentence containing a singular or plural possessive

5. Locate a series of pictures or illustrations on a given theme or topic.	Then use these as springboards for creating a series of "Pretend you are a …" situations for students to respond to. One teacher created these "pretend" statements for a set of pictures on the topic of "energy."
	
	Pretend you are a motorist and your gas tank is empty. The only gas station around has a "No Gas" sign out front.
	    Write a question you might ask the gas station attendant.
	    Write a statement you might say to a friend in the car with you.
	    Write a command to the car you are riding in.
	
	Pretend you are a light bulb in a lamp. You have been left on all night by mistake.
	    Write a question you might ask of the table your lamp is on.
	    Write a command to the owner of the house.
	    Write an exclamation to express how you feel at this moment.
	
	Pretend you are a nuclear reactor. People in your neighborhood don't want you there.
	    Write a question to the people who built you there.
	    Write a statement to the people who live in your neighborhood.
	    Write a command to the people who make you work.
	
	Pretend you are a solar heating system for a swimming pool on a dark and gloomy day.
	    Write a command to the sun.
	    Write a question to your owner.
	    Write an exclamation to express how you feel about your job.
	    Write a statement to the people who installed you.

6. Instruct students to locate ten illustrations from magazines that appear to be unrelated in terms of theme or content.	Once they have collected ten pictures, have them look for a theme amongst them all and write a story, essay, or mini–report from the picture collection.
7. Put students into cooperative learning groups of 8 people.	Instruct each person in each group to bring in a magazine illustration of an adult person mounted on a piece of blank writing paper. Each student gives the person in his/her picture a name and writes it on the first line of the writing paper. Students then pass their pictures to the right and the next student adds the age and occupation of the person and again passes the paper to the right. This process is continued until all eight people have recorded the following information for each picture:
	a. marital status and size of family
	b. address and type of residence
	c. special hobbies, interests, or leisure time activities
	d. description of pet peeve
	e. description of recent award or accomplishment
	f. description of secret ambition
	Each student should limit his/her comments to one good sentence. After all students have written their responses on all eight "people pictures," have the students do one of the following tasks:
	a. Assume the role of that person and write a description of a typical day in his/her life.
	b. Assume the role of that person and together with the other members of the group "act out" a situation where all characters meet together at a school board meeting, at an outdoor concert, at an airport, in a hospital lounge, or in a court of law.
8. Bring in a selection of magazine illustrations representing many different subjects, situations, and events.	Number each picture and lay them face up on a large table or counter top. Instruct each student to pick out one of the pictures they like, but they are not to reveal their choice to anyone at this time. Next, have students volunteer to come forward one at a time and take the picture of their choice. Ask each person to spend 2–3 minutes telling the class why he/she picked the picture, what things about it are appealing, and what emotions the picture evokes.

3. Dialogue Do's for Improving Discussions

Effective for students who:

- learn best in an auditory setting.
- exhibit strength in linguistic intelligence.
- require active involvement in lecture or discussion setting

 Use the following techniques to improve both the dialogue and interaction of students during small and large group discussion settings.

1. Initiate a discussion by having students respond to an open–ended question individually and then share their ideas with a partner before discussing responses with the whole group.

2. Organize a discussion by having each student or small group of students write out a question or concern they have about the topic for discussion on individual file cards. Collect the cards and use these student–generated ideas as the sole basis for the discussion session.

3. Stop the large group dialogue at several points during a discussion and instruct students to discuss this "last major point" with a partner or small group.

4. Pause during a discussion session and survey students to determine how they feel about a question that has just been answered or a point that has just been raised by a peer. For example, you might ask: "How many of you agree with the answer just given by John?" or "Raise your hand if you think this point made by Susan is an important one to consider."

5. Provide each student or pair of students in a discussion group with a response tool such as a set of prescribed Yes/No cards, individual chalkboards, or set of A, B, C, D multiple choice sheets of paper. After asking a question, instruct students to signal their answers by showing you the best "response" on their prop or response manipulative tool.

6. Keep students on their toes during discussion by tossing a ball to a student after asking a question. Whoever catches the ball must respond to the question.

7. Ask several relevant questions of the students during a discussion and propose several different answers to each question. Have students respond to each set of questions/answers by demonstrating one of the following "body language" techniques:

a. Stand up if you think "A" is the best answer.

b. Thumbs up if your think "B" is the best answer.

c. Raise your right hand if you think "C" is the best answer.

d. Raise your left hand if you think "D" is the best answer.

8. Fist of Five
   To use this strategy, the teacher poses a series of discussion statements, facts, opinions, or decisions and asks each member of the class to respond to each idea by using a "fist of five." The student responds to the idea by doing one of the following:

a. Raise hand as fist to indicate: *Do not agree with idea and will block idea*

b. Raise one finger to indicate: *Do not agree with idea but will not block idea*

c. Raise two fingers to indicate: *Am neutral on idea*

d. Raise three fingers to indicate: *Agree with this idea*

e. Raise four fingers to indicate: *Agree with this idea and will actively support idea*

f. Raise five fingers to indicate: *Agree with this idea and will lead the charge/action/ discussion on this idea*

Refill as often as necessary

4. Ten Ways to Write a Report That Can't Fail

Effective for students who:

- read and write below grade level
- become easily bored with research tasks
- vary in academic ability

 Introduce students to one or more of the following organizational schemata for structuring a report in any subject area.

 Show students how to collect and write out their factual information according to the letters of the alphabet. Students should create one fact that begins with each letter of the alphabet. You may want to give them the option of selecting any 12 letters of the alphabet, of eliminating any 5 letters of the alphabet, or of earning bonus points for using all letters of the alphabet.

 Show students how to use numbers as the basis for researching information and presenting their ideas in a numerical structure. For example, students might choose to write a report on a country and organize their ideas in this way:

- TEN Important Dates in German History
- NINE Key Cities to Know Something About in Germany
- EIGHT German Tourist Attractions to Visit
- SEVEN Famous German Artists, Poets, Writers, or Composers
- SIX Foods Popular with German Citizens
- FIVE Geographical Facts About Germany's Location
- FOUR German Words to Know and Use
- THREE Reasons to Study the German Culture
- TWO Problems the German Government is Trying to Solve
- ONE Little Known Fact About Germany's People

Bookmark Report

Show students a variety of bookmark samples that can be obtained at little or no cost from most book stores. Many retail outlets print up bookmarks that advertise new book releases and give information about the author or the content. Have students select a topic and create a set of informational bookmarks on that topic. Each bookmark should cover one major theme of the topic and all themes/bookmarks should be related to one another. For example, a student might choose to report on rocks and minerals, and the bookmark themes might include an informational bookmark on sedimentary rocks, one on metamorphic rocks, one on igneous rocks, one on fossils, one on minerals, and one on precious gems.

Deck of Cards Report

Show students how they might construct a deck of cards as a reporting format. There are several ways to do this. A report of famous explorers, inventors, authors, mathematicians, composers, artists, U.S. Presidents, or world leaders might follow the baseball card model. A picture or sketch on the front and statistics, data, and facts on the back of each card are included. A report on insects might follow the RUM playing card model. Sets of cards on different insects might be created so that the backs of all cards have a common insect design but the fronts of all cards have a series of different insect species with relevant information about each one. A deck of 52 cards is created with 13 different insects/information passages so that each insect is repeated 4 times in accordance with the rules for playing RUMMY. Students use the cards to play the game (get all 4 insects of same card to make a run) and learn something about insects.

Poetry Report

Introduce students to some common poetry forms such as *haiku, diamante, tanka, lanterne, limerick, free verse,* and *concrete poems* as well as some common poetry terms such as *simile, personification, alliteration, metaphor, hyperbole,* and *onomatopoeia.* Have them select a topic for a report and try to use these poetry forms and terms as information sources on the topic. They might want to title their report something like: "Six Ways to Look at Outer Space." They could then select several poetry forms or terms to convey ideas from their space research such as:

- *Personification Example:* Personify John Glenn's space capsule by giving it several human qualities.

- *Simile Example:* Traveling through space is as peaceful as gliding through the sky in a hot air balloon.

- *Alliteration Example:* Soaring in space seems so scary and so spooky but surely has secrets to share with society.

- *Japanese Lantern Example:* Poetry pattern that is based on the arrangement of syllables with a pattern of 1–2–3–4–1. You can join several verse patterns together to form a more complete message.

- *Original Example:* Students may even want to invent their own poetry forms by establishing an original formula or pattern such as:

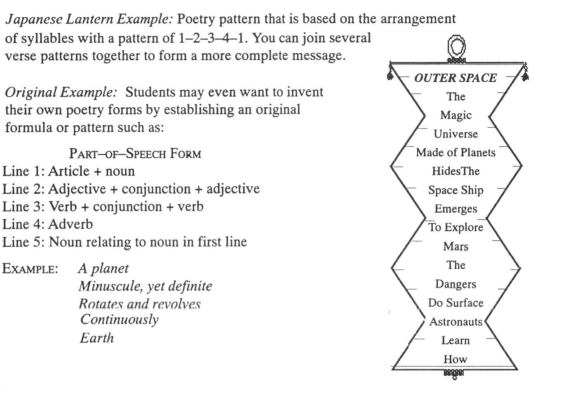

PART–OF–SPEECH FORM
Line 1: Article + noun
Line 2: Adjective + conjunction + adjective
Line 3: Verb + conjunction + verb
Line 4: Adverb
Line 5: Noun relating to noun in first line

EXAMPLE: *A planet*
             Minuscule, yet definite
             Rotates and revolves
             Continuously
             Earth

Note: Personification is especially effective as a report writing tool and can be adapted very easily to any subject area. Consider having your students write about:

A Day in the Life of a Snake Shedding its Skin

A Day in the Life of a Spider Building a Web

A Day in the Life of a Stop Watch at the Olympics

A Day in the Life of a Kettle in a Homeless Shelter

A Day in the Life of a Dictionary in a Publishing House

A Day in the Life of a Word Processor at City Hall

A Day in the Life of a Globe with a Travel Agent

A Day in the Life of a Microscope in a Hospital Lab

Question & Answer Report

Show students how to construct a simple flip or accordion book format. Flip books have a series of pages stapled together at the top with each page at the bottom being one inch longer than its preceding page. Accordion books have their pages folded back and forth like an accordion so that each page has a front and back and so that the book becomes free standing. Students generate a list of ten questions on a topic of their choice.

They conduct research to find answers to these questions and write their findings up in a concise, but informative paragraph. Students write one question in the bottom margin of each flip book page so that one question appears on each page. The paragraphs with answers are then written on the top half of the appropriate page. In the accordion book format, students write a question on the front of each section with its corresponding paragraph on the back of the section. Students will want to reserve the first page of the flip book or the first section of the accordion book as the title page for the report.

Fact File Report

Explain to students that a fact file consists of a small recipe or file type box filled with 3 x 5 file cards that contain a series of informational statements and data compiled from research on a topic of one's choice. Dividers can be added to the collection of file cards as an organizing device so that fact cards are categorized in some meaningful way. For example, if a student is doing a report on the Revolutionary War for social studies, he/she would collect information about the Revolutionary War writing down a summary paragraph, a list, a chart/graph, or a diagram on each file card. These information cards, when completed, might then be divided into such categories as: Famous Battles, Causes, Important Dates/Events, Leaders, Issues, and Outcomes. Students could then take out each category of information cards and synthesize them to write one section of the final report, or the report can be submitted as a set of facts arranged in some logical order that makes sense to the student.

Eight Square Comic Report

Ask students to take a large sheet of newsprint, manilla drawing paper, or chart paper and fold it into eight squares. Students then write their report in such a way that one paragraph of information goes into each square along with some type of illustration or graphic, comic strip style.

Students are introduced to the various sections and/or types of articles most commonly found in the newspaper including news stories, feature stories, editorials, classified ads, display ads, book/movie reviews, stock market charts, etc. Students then select a topic to research and write up their information in a "king–size" front page format made from a large strip of shelf paper. Information is presented on that king–size front page in a variety of newspaper formats ranging from news and feature stories to editorials and cartoons.

Students use a shoe box to collect or draw a set of artifacts that relate to a person or topic that they are researching. These artifacts can be actual small items, pictures, symbols, diagrams, charts, photographs, or sketches that have some significant relationship to the topic under study. Students label and number each artifact in the box and one–by–one use these items as springboards for writing paragraphs of explanation or giving short talks of information.

Refill as often as necessary

5. Catalogs as Instructional Tools

Effective for students who:

- are visual and kinesthetic learners
- enjoy hands–on assignments
- prefer alternatives to the textbook
- display varied interests and abilities
- exhibit strength in spatial intelligence

 Catalogs present both teachers and students with valuable tools for teaching and learning basic skills in any subject area. It is important to begin collecting all types of catalogs before attempting to use them in any significant way. Setting up a "CATALOG LEARNING STATION or LIBRARY" is important because it provides students with many alternative catalog types that can cater to a variety of personal interests, consumer habits, and formats. Students can be of great help in contributing catalog resources that come to their homes as junk mail or that can be picked up at retail outlets throughout the community.

Some good catalogs to have:
- catalogs from major department stores such as Sears, Penney's, or Spiegel Company.
- specialty catalogs such as *The Chocolate Catalog* or *The Disney Catalog*.
- travel agency catalogs.
- humor–laden catalogs such as *The Catalog for Cat Owners* or *The Pigmania Catalog*.
- library collections of catalogs.
- toy catalogs.
- holiday catalogs.
- old–fashioned or historical catalogs.

Once the classroom catalog collection is in order, the teacher should spend time having students explore and identify the special and common features of catalogs such as:
- rich and colorful pictures and displays.
- items grouped by categories.
- attractive covers, layouts, print types, sizes, and paper.
- use of strong action verbs and colorful adjectives.
- creation of special images.
- precision of language due to limited copy space for each item.

Next the teacher should plan a variety of activities that use the catalogs to teach basic skills. Some ideas to consider include:

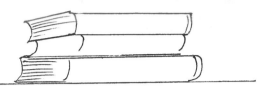

- planning a shopping spree for a special event.
- making wise consumer choices within a limited budget.
- preparing for one's own birthday or holiday celebration.
- locating "best" and "worst" values in selected categories of items for sale.
- figuring costs, orders, and sale prices or discounts.
- figuring sales taxes and shipping costs.
- analyzing colorful and figurative language common in advertising and display copy.
- drawing conclusions about word selections that are appealing to prospective buyers.

Finally, the teacher should encourage students to create special catalogs of their own on a topic related to one's course content. Examples to consider:

- a fairy tale catalog of items from popular stories such as Cinderella's glass slipper or a basket of treats for Little Red Riding Hood.
- a catalog for pioneer life complete with items for surviving on the wild frontier.
- a catalog for meteorologists that contains all types of weather predicting instruments.
- a catalog for number maniacs that feature everything from calculators and compasses to protractors and slide rules.

BONUS IDEA: Betty Klein of Lawton, Oklahoma, suggests using catalogs and story starting index cards in a creative writing center. The student selects an index card and then follows the directions on the card. The front side tells the student what types of items or people to cut out and glue on his/her story cover. The backside of the index card tells the student how to involve these items in a story. Two examples follow:

EXAMPLE #1

Front: Cut and glue pictures of 2 people in overcoats.
Back: These two people are spies for another country. They are here in the United States on special assignment and are meeting and giving each other a secret message.
Student Assignment: What are the spies' code names? What country are they from and what special assignment are they trying to carry out in the U.S.? What is the secret password? How are they exchanging the secret message? Is their mission a success?

EXAMPLE #2

Front: Cut and glue pictures of 3 pieces of sports equipment and 1 person.
Back: This person has just won an athletic event.
Student Assignment: What was the name of the team or person this individual defeated? If a team, what were the colors, fight song, and crucial play? If an individual, what did this person do in the event or training that enabled him/her to defeat his opponent? What is this person's name and background? How does everyone react to this victory?

---

6. Language Patterns That Lend Themselves to Writing Across the Content Areas

Effective for students who:

- have English as a second language
- represent diverse cultures
- are auditory learners
- exhibit strength in linguistic intelligence

Introduce students to a variety of language patterns that come from children's picture books or that teachers make up themselves. Share these language patterns with students and let them substitute their own words and phrases to the patterns making up original sentences with informational facts in a given subject area.

LANGUAGE PATTERN ONE: "The Important Thing" based on *The Important Book* by Margaret Wise Brown.

The important thing about a machine is that it helps us do more work with less effort.
— It has levers to pry things open and to cut things.
— It has pulleys to lift a load.
— It has inclined planes to help slide heavy things down a slope.

But, the important thing about a machine is that it helps us do more work with less effort.

The important thing about the Civil War is that it abolished slavery.
— It was caused by differences in the social structure and economy of the North and South.
— It cost more American lives than any other war in history.
— It led to the Emancipation Proclamation and the Gettysburg Address.

But, the important thing about the Civil War is that it abolished slavery.

LANGUAGE PATTERN TWO: " Money" based on the poem by Richard Armour.

MONEY

Workers earn it,
Spendthrifts burn it,
Bankers lend it,
Women spend it,
Forgers fake it,
Taxes take it,
Dying leave it,
Heirs receive it,
Thrifty save it,
Misers crave it,
Robbers seize it,
Rich increase it,
Gamblers lose it,
I could use it.

FOOD

Farmers grow it,
Manufacturers package it,
Supermarkets sell it,
Shoppers buy it,
Homeless crave it,
Children waste it,
Cooks prepare it,
Droughts destroy it,
Dieticians analyze it,
Dieters reject it,
People eat it,
I sure enjoy it.

LANGUAGE PATTERN THREE: I Used To . . . But Now I . . .

I used to think that animals were just like plants,
    …but now I know animals are unlike plants because they
cannot produce their own food from sunlight.

I used to think that animals were just like plants,
    …but now I know that they are unlike plants because they
can move around freely from place to place.

I used to think that animals were just like plants,
    …but now I know that they are unlike plants because they
can help rid the planet of waste by gobbling garbage and
dead plants and animals.

I used to think that if you lived in Ancient Egypt you lived in
apartment buildings,
    …but now I know you lived in villas.

I used to think that if you lived in Ancient Egypt you worked in
    factories,
    …but now I know you worked as farmers and craftspeople.

I used to think that if you lived in Ancient Egypt you rode around in cars,
    …but now I know you rode around on the Nile in boats.

LANGUAGE PATTERN FOUR: This language pattern is based on the book *What Do You Do With a Kangaroo?* by Mercer Mayer. It begins each page with the pattern: "What do you do with a Kangaroo who . . ." and the next page gives a logical response that begins with "You . . ." This pattern could be adapted to any content area for purposes of sharing information. Two examples below have been done to further illustrate the pattern.

What do you do with people who litter the parks and beaches with empty bottles or cans and say, "It's not my job to clean up the environment." You say that rubbish can be sorted and recycled and over half the aluminum drink cans in the USA are melted down and recycled.

What do you do with paper companies who insist on cutting down more trees than they need and say, "We plant trees for every one we cut down to help preserve our natural forests." You say it takes much longer to grow a tree than to cut one down and 35 million trees could be saved each year, if 75 per cent of waste paper and cardboard were recycled into pulp and used to make new paper.

LANGUAGE PATTERN FIVE: Another language pattern that works well for middle level students is one by Janice May Udry entitled "A Tree Is Nice." The pattern features a series of basic starter statements such as: A tree is nice for . . .; A tree is nice because . . .; A tree is nice to . . .; and A tree is nice since . . . Again, this can serve as a series of springboards for reporting pieces of information on a given subject. An example in science might be:

A diamond is nice because it is found in a rainbow of colors such as white, yellow, pink, green, blue, brown, red, and black. A diamond is nice to cut and polish so as to make it glitter. A diamond is nice for making into cutting tools. A diamond is nice since it is a rarity and known as a precious gemstone.

Refill as often as necessary

7. Fact and Focus

Effective for students who:

- are good critical and creative thinkers
- are interested in relationships among ideas

Prepare a set of facts to be learned, discussed, or reflected upon by students on any given topic important to a given subject area. After each fact, design a creative or critical thinking task related to the fact but also one that views the fact from a unique or unusual perspective.

EXAMPLE ONE: Plants: The Magic Food Source

Fact: Without green plants, life on Earth could not exist because we rely on green plants for food, clothing, shelter, and the air we breathe.

Focus: Design a special calendar around the theme of plants. For each month of the year, select a different plant or flower that seems appropriate. Draw, photograph, or find an illustration of the plant and write a short paragraph about it.

Fact: All living things use energy from food to keep them alive. Green plants are able to use sunlight to make their own food through a process called photosynthesis. One of the "waste" products of photosynthesis is oxygen, which the plant releases into the air you breathe.

Focus: Design a factory that manufactures plants. Begin with a seed which enters the factory through the front door and a full grown plant which exits the factory through the shipping and loading dock. What departments would the factory need and what would they look like?

Fact: Roots are an important part of the plant structure. They anchor the plant in the soil or onto a branch where the plant is growing. They also take in the water and dissolved minerals which a plant needs to make its food.

Focus: Draw a simple diagram to show your family "roots." Be able to explain how these "roots" are similar to the roots of a plant.

Fact: Members of the plant kingdom are divided into several main groups which are: Mosses and Liverworts, Ferns and Horsetails, Conifers, and Flowering Plants. The plants in each group share certain features such as where they live, what they look like, and how they reproduce.

Focus: Research to learn more about the plant kingdom and use the results to create a "planet dance" of movements representative of the various plant groups.

EXAMPLE TWO: Geometry

Fact: Geometry is the branch of mathematics that explains the relationship of points, lines, planes, and shapes to one another. Plane geometry is the study of two dimensional shapes or figures such as circles, squares, and triangles. Plane figures have only length and width. Solid geometry is the study of three– dimensional shapes such as cubes, spheres, and prisms. They have a third dimension which is height, or sometimes, depth.

Focus: Work with a small group of peers and create a series of different geometrical shapes with your bodies or create a skit in which the characters are various geometric shapes.

Fact: Three common types of angles that one will learn about in geometry are right angles that measure exactly 90 degrees, acute angles that measure less than 90 degrees and obtuse angles that measure more than 90 degrees but less than 180 degrees. A straight angle measures 180 degrees. Angles are commonly measured with a tool called a protractor.

Focus: Are you more like a right angle, straight angle, acute angle, or obtuse angle? Give several reasons for your answer.

Fact: Circles are geometric shapes that have no beginning or end. The area around the outside of the circle is called its circumference and the distance across the center of the circle is called its diameter.

Focus: Using only circles, create a wallpaper, wrapping paper, or fabric design. Experiment with a compass to help you with this task.

Refill as often as necessary

8. Clues to Reconstructing the Facts

Effective for students who:

- vary in reading ability
- are visual learners
- enjoy problem solving tasks
- exhibit strength in bodily–kinesthetic intelligence

 In this activity, the teacher prepares a set of artifacts, referred to as clues, around a given topic, theme, or set of concepts. These artifacts can range from a set of written clues in varying formats (letters, telephone messages, flyer, receipt or sales slip, newspaper article etc.) to a set of representative objects (tool, booklet, poster, souvenir, etc.). The students then use these clues or artifacts to produce an end product such as a written description or skit that summarizes the situation according to their synthesis of information presented through these clues. The teacher should also create a set of discussion questions and follow–up activities that can be used to guide the students in their investigations.

The following pages show an example of this strategy for a reading group that includes a set of clues, a synopsis of the situation, a set of discussion questions, and a set of follow–up activities. It is entitled "The Winning Entry." In addition, four outlines for other applications of this strategy that the teacher might want to do for practice are included.

Refill as often as necessary

4/4/94

Dear Sis,
    Sorry you couldn't
be here with mom, dad,
and me because we're
having a great time.
Will bring you a
surprise from Disney
World for helping me
with my research.
What size do you wear?
        Love, Jim
                sangamon

PS. Hope things are going well at school. See you soon!

Sally Reynolds
Univ. of Michigan
Room 220
Alice Lloyd Dorm
Ann Arbor, MI

        23260

STAMP

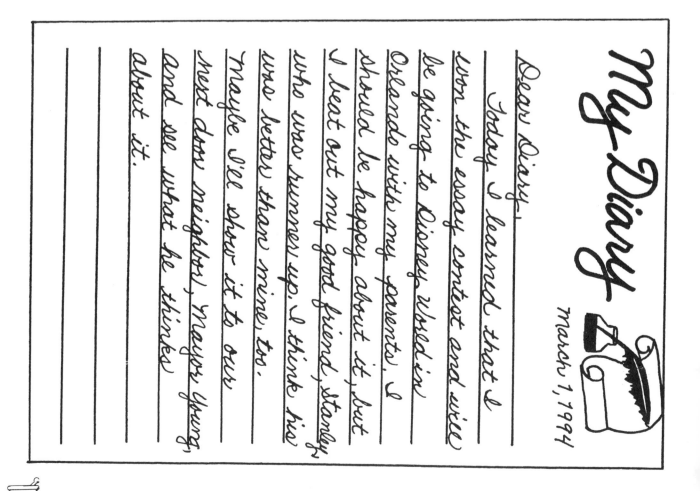

My Diary
march 1, 1994

Dear Diary,
    Today I learned that I
won the essay contest and will
be going to Disney World in
Orlando with my parents. I
should be happy about it, but
I beat out my good friend, Stanley,
who was runner up. I think his
was better than mine, too.
Maybe I'll show it to our
next door neighbor, Mayor Young,
and see what he thinks
about it.

24

Receipt (sales form):

Date April 6 1994

Mr. Tim Reynolds

No. Tampa, Florida

Reg. No. _____ Clerk _____ | ACCOUNT FORWARDED |

1			
2	1 Boy's Tee Shirt		
3	medium	7	00
4			
5	1 Lady's Tee Shirt		
6	medium	7	00
7			
8	PAID		
9		14	00
10	Tax		84
000315-10		14	84

YOUR ACCOUNT STATED TO DATE. RETURN AT ONCE IF ERROR IS FOUND

Receipt:

Date March 30 1994   No. 1

Received from University of So. Florida

$ 500.06   Dollars

☐ For Rent of _____ From ___ 19 ___ To ___ 19 ___

☒ For Cash for Expenses ; Trip to Disney World April 4-6, 1994

$ 500.00   By John & Joan Reynolds

Letter:

Dear Tim,

I just heard that you won the essay contest and I'm glad it's you if it couldn't be me. Bring me back a souvenir.

A disappointed buddy
S. Jones

Important Message:

IMPORTANT MESSAGE

FOR Tim Reynolds

DATE 3/1/94   TIME 4:30 (A.M. / P.M.)

M rs. Bentley

OF West Hills Middle School

PHONE _____

AREA CODE   NUMBER   EXTENSION

TELEPHONED		PLEASE CALL	
CAME TO SEE YOU		WILL CALL AGAIN	X
WANTS TO SEE YOU		RUSH	
RETURNED YOUR CALL		SPECIAL ATTENTION	

MESSAGE You did it! Congratulations on your social studies essay.

SIGNED Lucy

LITHO USA

TOPS ◆ FORM 3002P

25

ESSAY CONTEST

TOPIC: The Right to Vote

WHO CAN ENTER?
Students - grades 6-9

SPONSORED BY:
Political Science Department
University of South Florida, Tampa, FL.

RULES:

• Write an essay of 1000 words on the topic listed above. All work must be original and signed by your social studies teacher.

• Submit to Dr. Jane Washington, Professor of Political Science, University of South Florida, no later than January 1, 1994. Winner will be notified by March 1, 1994.

• Winner will receive an all expense paid weekend at Disney World for entrant and his/her parents.

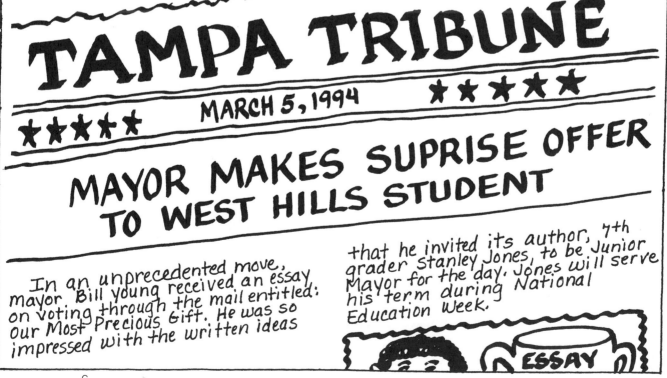

TAMPA TRIBUNE

★★★★★ MARCH 5, 1994 ★★★★★

MAYOR MAKES SUPRISE OFFER TO WEST HILLS STUDENT

In an unprecedented move, mayor Bill young received an essay on voting through the mail entitled: our Most Precious Gift. He was so impressed with the written ideas that he invited its author, 7th grader Stanley Jones, to be Junior Mayor for the day. Jones will serve his term during National Education Week.

ESSAY

Our Most Precious Gift

I. The 18-year old vote

A. When it become a law

B Why it became a law

II. Teen-age voting record

A. Election results of 1988

B. Election results of 1992

III. Voting as a privilege

IV. Voting as a responsibility

By Stanley Jones

National Resource Center
for Middle Grades Education
College of Education
University of South Florida
4202 East Fowler Avenue, EDU 118
Tampa, Florida 33520-5650
(813) 974-2530

February 28, 1994

Mr. Tim Reynolds
1600 Lakeview
Tampa, Florida 34506

Dear Tim,

The University of South Florida is pleased to announce that you are the first place winner of our annual essay contest on American Government.

You have won an all expense paid trip to Disney World for you and your parents on April 4-6, 1994.

On behalf of the judges, congratulations and keep up the good work.

Sincerely,

Dr. Jane Washington
Political Science Professor

JMW/lms

TAMPA   ST. PETERSBURG   SARASOTA   FORT MYERS   LAKELAND
UNIVERSITY OF SOUTH FLORIDA IS AN AFFIRMATIVE ACTION EQUAL OPPORTUNITY INSTITUTION

THE WINNING ENTRY

CHARACTERS

Tim Reynolds, age 13
Joan Reynolds, mother
Stan Jones, age 13
Dr. Jane Washington, professor

Sally Reynolds, age 19
John Reynolds, father
Mr. Bill Young, mayor
Mrs. Bently, social studies teacher

SYNOPSIS

Tim Reynolds has just won an expense paid trip for him and his parents to Disney World in Orlando, Florida, as a result of winning an essay contest. He has mixed emotions about the honor because he beat out his best friend, Stan Jones, who was runner up. Thanks to the help of the city mayor, though, all turns out well for both Tim and his friend.

VOCABULARY

privilege
political science
mock

responsibility
election
unprecedented

CLUES (10 items)

Telephone message
Personal note
Post card
Receipt
Sales slip

Journal entry
Outline for essay
Contest flyer
Newspaper article
Letter from University of South Florida

DISCUSSION QUESTIONS

1. Describe the clues at which you are looking.

2. Are any of he clues related? If so, which ones? In what ways?

3. Arrange the clues in the order that the events seem to have happened. Explain why you arranged them that way. Are there any other ways in which you could arrange them?

4. In one or two sentences, tell the main idea of this clue's story.

5. What effect do you think Stan's notes had on Tim, if any?

THE WINNING ENTRY (continued)

6.   Which clues could be placed in a category labeled "Good News." Give reasons for your choices.

7.   What type of person do you think the main character is and why?

8.   What did Stan Jones write about for his essay?

FOLLOW-UP ACTIVITIES

1.   Create some additional clues for the story that might change or alter the plot in some way.

2.   Present a mock television newscast interviewing Tim Reynolds upon his return from Disney World.

3.   Present a mock television newscast interviewing Stan Jones upon completion of his day as Junior Mayor of the City.

4.   Design an essay contest with your own suggested topic, rules, and prizes.

5.   Plan a skit to act out this story the way you think it happened.

6.   Use Stan Jones's outline to write a short essay on voting.

TITLE _____

CHARACTERS

_____   _____

_____   _____

_____   _____

SYNOPSIS

Susan Carter was a non-English speaking student in a predominately white school. She had moved to the U.S. from Mexico after her father had received his official papers as a legal alien. She was placed in a part-time special program for minorities at her middle school to receive special help in learning the language. After three months in the States, she was surprised to win a special New Student Achievement Award from her teacher. The students in her regular classes were proud of her and let her know it.

VOCABULARY

_____   _____

_____   _____

_____   _____

CLUES (10 items)

_____   _____

_____   _____

_____   _____

_____   _____

_____   _____

DISCUSSION QUESTIONS

_____

_____

_____

FOLLOW-UP ACTIVITIES

_____

TITLE _____

CHARACTERS

_____   _____

_____   _____

_____   _____

SYNOPSIS

Tim Barker was just elected President of the Student Council at Kennedy Middle School after a close election with three other candidates. His platform was centered around the need for more computers in the classroom. He involved IBM from the business community and a local school board member from the district in his campaign. As a result of his successful campaign, Tom was honored at a special Junior Achievement Recognition Dinner sponsored by the school PTA.

VOCABULARY

_____   _____

_____   _____

_____   _____

CLUES (10 items)

_____   _____

_____   _____

_____   _____

_____   _____

DISCUSSION QUESTIONS

_____

_____

_____

FOLLOW-UP ACTIVITIES

_____

TITLE _____

CHARACTERS

_____   _____

_____   _____

_____   _____

SYNOPSIS

Kim Hopkins, an eighth grader, had always been a good student until recently. She got involved with an older group of high school dropouts and began skipping school. Her parents sought professional help for her at school and in the community to turn things around. Several incidents happened at one time to make Kim respond positively to the advice she was given.

VOCABULARY

_____   _____

_____   _____

_____   _____

CLUES (10 items)

_____   _____

_____   _____

_____   _____

_____   _____

_____   _____

DISCUSSION QUESTIONS

_____

_____

_____

FOLLOW-UP ACTIVITIES

_____

TITLE _____

CHARACTERS

_____   _____

_____   _____

_____   _____

SYNOPSIS

John Watson was a seventh grader whose father had just lost his job. John's mother was ill and required expensive medical treatment. His older sisters, Beth and Sarah, were in high school in a work coop program which allowed them to earn all their spending money and help defray family expenses. John wanted a job too and set out to find legitimate work. At first he was unsuccessful but later got work for both his father and himself.

VOCABULARY

_____   _____

_____   _____

_____   _____

CLUES (10 items)

_____   _____

_____   _____

_____   _____

_____   _____

_____   _____

DISCUSSION QUESTIONS

_____

_____

_____

FOLLOW-UP ACTIVITIES

_____

33

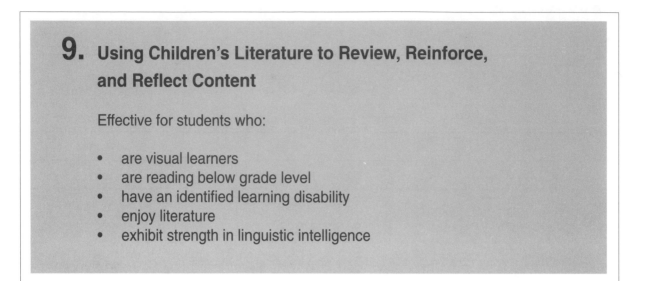

9. Using Children's Literature to Review, Reinforce, and Reflect Content

Effective for students who:

- are visual learners
- are reading below grade level
- have an identified learning disability
- enjoy literature
- exhibit strength in linguistic intelligence

 Visit the picture book section of the local elementary school or community public library to identify a number of books that are related to a topic that is being studied in a given discipline. Prepare a series of student directed "file folders" for each of the selected picture books that require the student to read the book and then react to the book's content. The outside front cover of the folder should have the title of the book along with the author, illustrator, publisher, and copyright date. The inside sections of the file folder should contain a synopsis of the story as well as directions for a series of related interdisciplinary tasks. The back cover of the file folder should have a reproducible page of six questions on the book that is based on Bloom's Taxonomy to focus on a wide range of thinking skill challenges. These "file folder" literature notes often help the student understand the relationship of a science, social studies, mathematical, or language arts concept to the world of literature. In short, this strategy helps the student to look at common things in uncommon ways.

Two sample "file folder" literature notes are included on the following pages. Other popular picture books that lend themselves to this approach are listed by subject area.

Refill as often as necessary

REPRODUCIBLE PAGE:
SAMPLE FILE FOLDER FOR *IF YOU MADE A MILLION*

OUTSIDE FRONT COVER: Title, Author, Illustrator, Publisher, and Copyright Date

IF YOU MADE A MILLION

by David M. Schwartz

pictures by Steven Kellogg
New York: Lothrop, Lee, & Shepard Books
Copyright ©1989

INSIDE FRONT AND BACK COVERS:

SYNOPSIS: Marvelosissimo the Mathematical Magician serves as a guide in this book for exploring the fascinating world of money. He introduces the reader to a wide variety of concepts including numerical values, banking procedures, interest on savings, and purchasing power.

MATHEMATICS

Devise a method or strategy for explaining/demonstrating the concept of 1,000,000 to a primary student.

ART

Create a magician puppet much like the wizard "Marvelosissimo" and use him to act out the major concepts in the story. You may even want to write an additional script or copy for the book focusing on other "money" related ideas that you could teach others using the magician puppet.

LANGUAGE ARTS

Brainstorm as many other things as you can think of besides stars that number in the millions. Write them down in list form and in alphabetical order. Next, brainstorm a list of things that are very small in number such as oceans or endangered species. Write these in alphabetical order. What conclusions can you draw from the items that appear on your two lists?

SOCIAL STUDIES

Research to find out how coins are manufactured at the U.S. Mint and bills are produced at the Bureau of Engraving. Write your findings up in a simple outline or diagram format.

CREATIVE WRITING

Write a humorous story about the problems a family or community has when they try to "barter" goods before the invention of money.

SCIENCE

Research to discover what types of metals are used in the minting of U.S. coins. What properties do they have and why were they chosen for this purpose? Are there other metals that could be used instead?

MATHEMATICS

Fill a container with a large number of some small item such as paper clips, M & M's, or marbles. Stage a contest for students in your class to guess or estimate the number of items in the container. Record their responses on a chart. Change the size of the container on a daily basis and have those same students guess or estimate the number of items in the new container. Do their estimation skills improve with practice?

CREATIVE THINKING

In your own words, explain the meaning of these famous money–related proverbs or quotations and decide whether you agree with them or not and why:

1. Early to bed and early to rise, makes a man happy, wealthy, and wise.
2. Without the love of books, the richest man is poor.
3. Making money is easy; knowing what to do with it becomes a problem.
4. Those who believe money can do everything are frequently prepared to do everything for money.
5. Everything in the world may be endured except continued prosperity.

CRITICAL THINKING

Do you agree with this person's analysis of one million dollars: "A million dollars is a sum that may be honestly acquired by putting aside five hundred dollars out of one's salary every week for forty years." Give reasons for your answer.

> *BONUS TASK:* Select five different–sized objects in the classroom and make guesses about how far one million of each object would reach using local geography as your ultimate yardstick. Then compute the answer by following this process: Measure each object's length in inches, multiply by 1,000,000; then divide the resulting number by 12 (to convert to feet) and again by 5,280 (to convert to miles). For example, a million paper clips, each 1 1/4" long would reach 20 miles or to our neighboring city, Tampa.

OUTSIDE BACK COVER:

KNOWLEDGE LEVEL: Define the concept of "interest" in economic terms as used in the book.

COMPREHENSION LEVEL: In a short essay, describe what you would do IF YOU MADE A MILLION DOLLARS!

APPLICATION: Write a series of "interest" generating word problems in math for others to solve. Be sure to include an answer key with the correct solutions.

ANALYSIS: Determine what techniques the authors have used to put abstract numerical concepts into recognizable terms for kids to learn and understand.

SYNTHESIS: Use your imagination to design one of the following original projects:

Option One: A king–size "piggy–type" bank or vault to hold a million dollars.
Option Two: A personalized checkbook and check design for you.
Option Three: A new currency and coin system for the U.S.

EVALUATION: Rank order the following occupations on a scale of 1 to 5 according to which are the most deserving of an annual salary that is one million dollars a year. Make 1 your most deserving and 5 your least deserving. Establish criteria for the decision and defend your first and last choices.

Occupations to consider:

Judge
Surgeon
College Professor
Scientist
Governor

REPRODUCIBLE PAGE: SAMPLE FILE FOLDER FOR *PEOPLE*

OUTSIDE FRONT COVER: Title, Author, Illustrator, Publisher, and Copyright Date

PEOPLE

written and illustrated by
Peter Spier
New York: Delacorte Press, Bantam Doubleday Dell
Publishing Group, Inc.
Copyright ©1980

INSIDE FRONT AND BACK COVERS:

SYNOPSIS: With more than four billion people in the world, author Peter Spier reminds us that each person is a unique individual, different from all others, and deserving of the respect and tolerance of others. He compares many different cultures by showing what different people look like, eat, celebrate, touch, and worship. His colorful illustrations convey both a sense of humor and a sense of hope.

SOCIAL STUDIES

Select a culture very different from your own and research information about it. Examine the culture's clothing, food, language, occupations, leisure time activities, housing, religion, celebrations, and geographical location. Write up your findings in a booklet or pamphlet format.

MATHEMATICS

Construct a series of bar graphs that relate to questions about *People.* First write a set of questions down on a piece of paper. Survey the class to find out their responses to the questions. Tally the results and draw a set of bar graphs that display the results. Some questions to consider might be:

Which picture or point of difference discussed in the book was your favorite?
What culture or ethnic background is most represented in your classroom?
Which pet described in the book seems the most exotic to you?

LANGUAGE ARTS

Pretend you could interview the author, Peter Spier. Write out a set of interview questions you would like to ask him. Give your questions to a friend and have him/her write out a set of potential responses. Use these questions and answers to stage a mock interview for the class.

SCIENCE

Human genetics is difficult to study for several reasons. First, a scientist cannot do experiments with humans. Secondly, the life span of humans is long so that a scientist cannot study all the offspring produced over generations in his/her own lifetime. Thirdly, humans produce few offspring which makes it hard to compare traits. We do know some things about heredity, however, and four of those facts are outlined on the following page.

Some Facts About Heredity
1. Traits are inherited.
2. Inherited traits are passed on from parents to offspring.
3. The way inherited traits are based is called heredity.
4. The modern science of heredity is called genetics.

Use your science book to locate information about one of the following topics and design a simple poster to show a summary of what you learned.
   a. What are inherited characteristics?
   b. Why are chromosomes important?
   c. Why can offspring look different from their parents?
   d. Can the environment affect inherited traits?
   e. How is genetics used to improve plants and animals?
   f. What is genetic engineering?

ART

Create a paper doll representative of a specific culture and design a fashion wardrobe of ethnic outfits for him/her to wear. Consider a paper doll from Japan, Mexico, Egypt, or Ancient Rome.

GEOGRAPHY

Plan a trip around the world where you visit at least one different city or country on each continent for a week. Write out your itinerary for each week long visit telling where you will go and what you will do.

READING

Visit the picture book section of your local elementary school or community library and compile an annotated bibliography of books that represent various cultures around the world.

OUTSIDE BACK COVER: Reproducible Page for *People*

KNOWLEDGE LEVEL: Record the author's purpose for writing this book according to the reviews on the back cover of the book or according to the description on the inside flap of the book's cover.

COMPREHEN-SION: In your own words, explain how this book could be called a "delicious treat for the senses."

APPLICATION: Construct a fact sheet or fact file of information you have gained about people from reading this book.

ANALYSIS: Determine why reviewers of this book, such as Jacques Cousteau, have called it a "smiling lesson of ecology."

SYNTHESIS: Create a memorial, monument, or marker to celebrate your accomplishments and to remember you long after you are gone.

EVALUATION: Defend or negate this statement: "It is in part the very uniqueness of every individual that makes him, not only a member of a family, race, nation, or class, but a human being."

PICTURE BOOKS WITH A MATH THEME

Arithmetic by Carl Sandburg and illustrated by Ted Rand. Harcourt Brace Jovanovich, Orlando, 1993.

An Illusionary Tale:OPT by Arline and Joseph Baum. Puffin Books, New York, 1989.

Mother Earth's Counting Book by Andrew Clements and illustrated by Lonni Sue Johnson. Picture Book Studio, Saxonville, MA, 1992.

Socrates and the Three Little Pigs by Tuyosi Mori and illustrated by Mitsumasa Anno. Philomel Books, New York, 1986.

12 Ways To Get To 11 by Eve Merriam and illustrated by Bernie Karlin. Simon & Schuster, New York, 1993.

PICTURE BOOKS WITH A SCIENCE THEME

Cloudy With a Chance of Meatballs by Judi Barrett and illustrations by Ron Barrett. Macmillan, New York, 1978.

Demi's Secret Garden by Demi. Henry Holt, New York, 1993.

Just A Dream by Chris Van Allsburg. Houghton Mifflin, Boston, 1990.

The Magic School Inside The Human Body (and other *Magic School Bus* titles) by Joanna Cole and illustrated by Bruce Degen. Scholastic, New York, 1989.

The Story of May by Mordicai Gerstein. Harper Collins, New York, 1993.

The Sun, the Wind, and the Rain by Lisa Westberg Peters and illustrated by Ted Rand. Henry Holt, New York, 1988.

PICTURE BOOKS WITH A LANGUAGE ARTS THEME

Cinder–Elly by Frances Minters and illustrated by G. Brian Karas. Viking Penguin, New York, 1994.

The Jolly Postman or Other People's Letters by Janet & Allan Ahlberg. Little, Brown and Company, Boston, 1986.

Many Luscious Lollipops (and other books on parts of speech by Ruth Heller) by Ruth Heller. Grosset & Dunlap, New York, 1989.

The True Story Of The 3 Little Pigs by A. Wolf as told to Jon Scieszka (and other books by Jon Scieszka) and illustrated by Lane Smith. Viking Penguin, New York, 1989.

PICTURE BOOKS WITH A SOCIAL STUDIES THEME

Baseball Saved Us by Ken Mochizuki and illustrated by Dom Lee. Lee & Low Books, New York, 1993.

The Giraffe That Walked To Paris by Nancy Milton and illustrated by Roger Roth. Crown Publishers, New York, 1992.

Oh, the Places You'll Go! by Dr. Seuss. Random House, New York, 1990.

Only Opal: The Diary of a Young Girl by Jane Boulton and illustrated by Barbara Cooney. Philomel Books, New York, 1994.

Talking Walls by Margy Burns Knight and illustrated by Anne Sibley O'Brien. Tilbury House, Gardiner, ME 1992.

The Wretched Stone by Chris Van Allsburg. Houghton Mifflin, Boston, 1991.

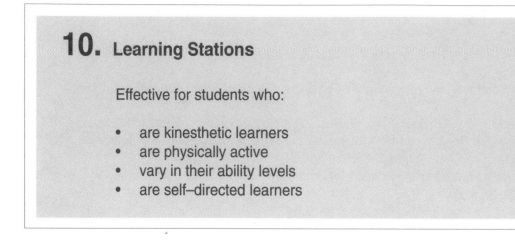

10. Learning Stations

Effective for students who:

- are kinesthetic learners
- are physically active
- vary in their ability levels
- are self–directed learners

 Learning stations provide students and teachers with many options for learning and applying basic skills in any subject area. They also encourage students to assume more responsibility for their own behavior in the acquisition of skills and information. Although there are many formats for developing and implementing learning station activities and management systems, the models described below are good for getting started with them in any middle level classroom. It is also suggested that the teacher design the learning center activities around a structure such as Bloom's Taxonomy, William's Taxonomy, or the Multiple Intelligences so that the learning tasks reflect a wide range of learning styles and thinking skills. Examples of these formats along with some tips for managing learning stations are included on the following pages.

Format one:

TASK CARDS

Develop simple sets of task cards on 5 x 8 file cards or 8 1/2 x 11 card stock sheets. Select a topic or theme to use as the basis for your learning station and use it as the organizing structure for the task cards. Decide on the number of tasks you wish to include and write out one task on each card or sheet. Add computer graphics or clip art to each card to stimulate visual interest and highlight important parts of the assigned task. These cards can be stored in a standard file box container for easy access and portability by students. A set of sample, reproducible task cards from an interdisciplinary unit in science entitled "Adventures in Reading, Writing, and Eating" is included on the following pages. Activity titles and suggestions for use are:

A Tour Guide Through The Food Tube
People Are What They Eat
What If Fast Food Restaurants Were Hazardous To Your Health
A Picture Is Worth A Thousand Words
To Buy Or Not To Buy ... That Is The Question
Containers Are Not Always What They Seem
Plan A Cooking Demonstration
Thin May Be In But Fat Is Where It's At
Dear Food Detective
Food For Thought

Format two:

MINI-DISPLAY BOARDS

Create a set of mini, three–sided display boards that are free standing from cardboard boxes or poster board. (They can also be purchased in various sizes from an office supply store). Each panel of the display board should be approximately 9" wide and 11" tall. Again, choose a theme or topic for the display board learning station. Write out descriptions of the tasks for students to do and mount them on cut–out shapes of construction paper. Paste these on the display board along with a title of cut–out letters to make the boards attractive and interesting. A sample display board for social studies using travel folders as the theme is included on the following pages. Like the task cards, these display boards are easily stored in a cupboard or file drawer and are portable for use at individual student desks or tables.

Format three:

ARTIFACT PACKAGES

Discovering or selecting an unusual container or packaging design can often be a stimulus for putting together a learning station. Examples that creative teachers have adapted using this approach include: Creating king–size chocolate kiss shapes with the student tasks printed on them that are stored in a chocolate tin for a station on "CHOCOLATE," creating king–size water droplets with the student tasks printed on them that are stored in an open umbrella for a station on "WEATHER," or writing student tasks on inside covers of department store gift boxes that are stored in a large and colorful shopping bag for a station on "CONSUMERISM." The sample learning station on consumerism in social studies is included on the following pages.

Format four:

**PHOTO ALBUMS
OR NOTEBOOKS
WITH PLASTIC
SLEEVES**

Printing learning center activities on paper with decorative borders, designs, or stick figures and then placing them in slots of a large photograph album or in individual plastic sleeve protectors is also an efficient method for creating work stations. This format becomes a learning station in a book and can contain several pages of activities which afford students more choices of what to do or teachers more space for designating specific activities for kids to do. The following pages contain a series of learning center tasks to familiarize students with the multimedia resources of a school library or media center. They were actually stored in a notebook in the media center and students completed them on a voluntary or assigned basis for extra credit when they had free time in the library.

Format five:

SHOES

Purchase some string tags. Buy the largest size. Write a shoe-related question or activity on each one and tie them in a bunch on an old shoe. You now have an instant moveable learning center. Students answer questions as seatwork or homework. Encourage students to bring an interesting shoe from home. Provide blank tags. Students compose questions. You now have 25 instant moveable learning centers! Sample questions for the tags are included on pages 60-61.

Refill as often as necessary

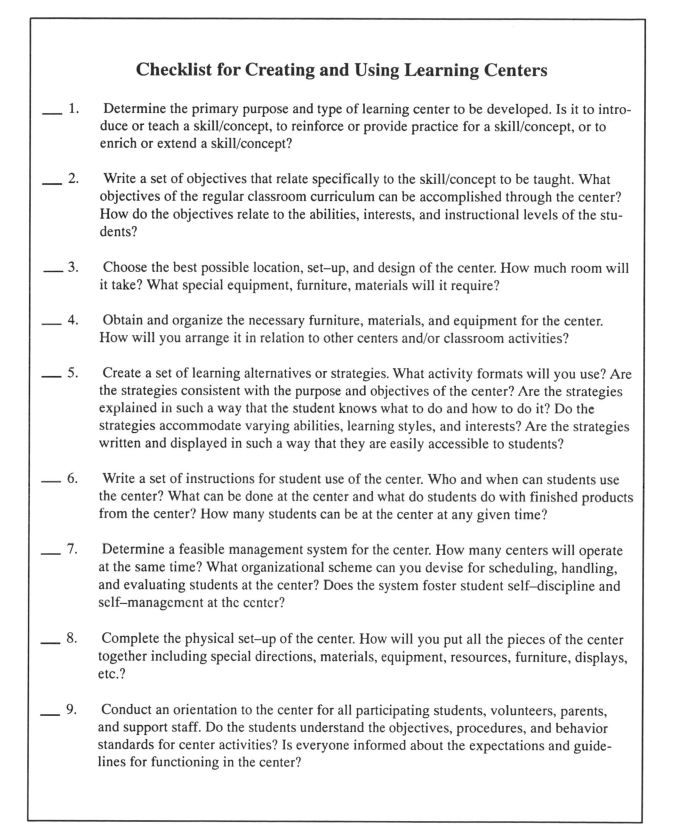

Checklist for Creating and Using Learning Centers

___ 1. Determine the primary purpose and type of learning center to be developed. Is it to introduce or teach a skill/concept, to reinforce or provide practice for a skill/concept, or to enrich or extend a skill/concept?

___ 2. Write a set of objectives that relate specifically to the skill/concept to be taught. What objectives of the regular classroom curriculum can be accomplished through the center? How do the objectives relate to the abilities, interests, and instructional levels of the students?

___ 3. Choose the best possible location, set–up, and design of the center. How much room will it take? What special equipment, furniture, materials will it require?

___ 4. Obtain and organize the necessary furniture, materials, and equipment for the center. How will you arrange it in relation to other centers and/or classroom activities?

___ 5. Create a set of learning alternatives or strategies. What activity formats will you use? Are the strategies consistent with the purpose and objectives of the center? Are the strategies explained in such a way that the student knows what to do and how to do it? Do the strategies accommodate varying abilities, learning styles, and interests? Are the strategies written and displayed in such a way that they are easily accessible to students?

___ 6. Write a set of instructions for student use of the center. Who and when can students use the center? What can be done at the center and what do students do with finished products from the center? How many students can be at the center at any given time?

___ 7. Determine a feasible management system for the center. How many centers will operate at the same time? What organizational scheme can you devise for scheduling, handling, and evaluating students at the center? Does the system foster student self–discipline and self–management at the center?

___ 8. Complete the physical set–up of the center. How will you put all the pieces of the center together including special directions, materials, equipment, resources, furniture, displays, etc.?

___ 9. Conduct an orientation to the center for all participating students, volunteers, parents, and support staff. Do the students understand the objectives, procedures, and behavior standards for center activities? Is everyone informed about the expectations and guidelines for functioning in the center?

A TOUR GUIDE THROUGH THE FOOD TUBE

Pretend you are a travel agent whose job it is to plan, promote, and conduct a guided tour of the digestive system. To prepare for this exciting responsibility, you must design an interesting and unique travel brochure that tells what one can expect to see and do while on this tour of the food tube. Be sure to include descriptions and diagrams of the important facts to be learned from this excursion.

PEOPLE ARE WHAT THEY EAT

Work with a small group of students to plan and video/audio tape a series of television/radio public service announcements that explain the many causes, dangers, symptoms, and treatments for such teenage eating disorders as anorexia, bulimia, obesity, anemia, and fad diets. Make each announcement factual, colorful, informative, and appealing to this age group.

WHAT IF FAST FOOD RESTAURANTS WERE HAZARDOUS TO YOUR HEALTH?

What if the Food and Drug Administration declared all fast food restaurants to be hazardous to your health? Record your thoughts about this situation by responding to the following questions in writing:

1. What is a health hazard?
2. Why might fast food restaurants be considered hazardous to your health?
3. How would the restaurant industry be affected?
4. How would people in your school and community react to this finding?
5. What arguments might you present to refute the premise that fast food restaurants are a health hazard?

A PICTURE IS WORTH A THOUSAND WORDS

Create a picture or photo essay that discusses the four food groups in detail and their importance to effective meal planning and nutrition. Be sure to add a caption to each picture you draw or snap with your camera.

OR

Show pictures you have drawn or have found in magazines on the four food groups and verbally explain their significance to effective meal planning and nutrition.

OR

Write and illustrate a children's picture book about the four food groups. Be sure to create an interesting title and cover for your book.

TO BUY OR NOT TO BUY ... THAT IS THE QUESTION

Conduct a survey of members in your class to determine how often they buy their lunch at school, bring their lunch to school, or skip their lunch in school and what factors are involved in making this decision. Graph your results.

OR

Conduct a survey of members in your class to determine their favorite lunch menu served and sold at school and their favorite lunch menu packed and brought to school. Graph your results.

OR

Conduct a survey of members in your class to determine whether junk food should be sold at school and, if so, what foods should receive priority on the junk food menu. Graph your results.

CONTAINERS ARE NOT ALWAYS WHAT THEY SEEM

A container is anything that can hold something within itself or within fixed limits. The supermarket is full of very unusual and unique food containers. Go on a supermarket treasure hunt and locate as many different types of containers as you can. Look for variety in shape, weight, material, size, and seal. Summarize your observations in a display, collage, or report. Then complete one of the following tasks:

1. Think of as many uses (besides storing food) as you can for a Pringle can.
2. Design a new container for a food product.
3. The perfect container is said to be the egg shell.
   Think about this statement and write a paragraph telling why you agree or disagree with it.
4. Create a poster to show how food containers add to the cost, convenience, and marketability of a product.

PLAN A COOKING DEMONSTRATION

A popular type of television show today is one that shares recipes and shows cooking techniques. Pretend you have been selected to serve as the "student chef" of a new kid show that focuses on easy recipes for today's busy teenager.

Locate a number of recipe books written for kids and by kids at your school or community media center. Select one or more recipes from these books that are simple, healthy, inexpensive, and fun to prepare

Plan a "live" cooking demonstration for your class to introduce your new television show. You might even want to prepare a mini-cookbook of these recipes to pass out at this time.

THIN MAY BE IN BUT FAT IS WHERE IT'S AT

Browse through a number of science reference books from the library or science textbooks from the classroom that contain a number of experiments with food. For example, discover how one might test foods for starch, foods for fats, foods for proteins, and foods for carbohydrates.

Conduct one or more of these food experiments and write up your findings in a learning log.

Next, examine the labels on a wide variety of food products you have in your home. Write down the types of information you most commonly find written on these labels. Do this in your learning log.

DEAR FOOD DETECTIVE

Create a question-and-answer column for your school or local newspaper that deals with health, nutrition, and fitness issues. Create a series of questions that could be submitted to such a column by its readers along with a set of sample responses for each one.

Prepare a Fact File of information on these topics that could be used as an information or reference source. Put your facts on 3X5 file cards with one or two major ideas on each card. Organize your cards according to some easy-to-find method.

FOOD FOR THOUGHT

Food items have sometimes been used as metaphors when creating figures of speech to make a point. Some examples are:

1. She needs to put some meat on her bones.
2. He is a chicken when it comes to trying new things.
3. His daughter is the apple of his eye.
4. It's like taking candy from a baby.
5. The movie was my cup of tea.
6. She is as cool as a cucumber.

In your own words, explain what is meant by each of these food expressions. Can you think of others to add to the examples above?

F IS FOR FOLDERS OF TRAVEL

KNOWLEDGE: Locate a number of travel folders representative of sights in your community or state. List them in alphabetical order.

COMPREHENSION: Summarize the main purpose of a travel folder and the types of information one is most likely to find in them.

APPLICATION: Use one of the travel folders in your collection and write out a set of comprehension questions that can be answered by reading the information in it.

ANALYSIS: Compare and contrast any two travel folders in the collections. How are they alike and how are they different?

SYNTHESIS: Redesign one of the travel folders in the collection so that it has a special appeal for kids your age.

EVALUATION: Conclude how travel folders are a type of propaganda.

TRAVEL FOLDER APPLICATION ACTIVITIES FOR ME TO DO

Create an unusual but informative travel folder for one of these special situations:

LANGUAGE ARTS: A Travel Folder for Storybook Land

SOCIAL STUDIES: A Travel Folder for a Trip Back in Time

MATH: A Travel Folder for a New Disney World Attraction called Geometry Junction.

SCIENCE: A Travel Folder for a Location in Outer Space

BONUS: Collect travel folders for tourist attractions in your community or state. Design a travel learning center for your class with these as springboards for activities.

T IS FOR . . . TRAVEL FOLDER

My Ideas About Travel Folders

1. Travel folders or brochures are most commonly found in such locations as

_____

_____

2. Travel folders help the consumer (buyer) most by

_____

_____

_____

3. Travel folders help the producer (seller) most by

_____

_____

_____

4. One word of caution I would give someone about using travel folders might be

_____

_____

5. Travel folders provide the individual with many different kinds of information including

_____

_____

_____

CONSUMERISM

1. DOLLARS: Interview at least 25 classmates to find out how they earn their allowance or spending money, how much they get or make, and what they spend it on. Record all responses. Graph your results to post in your classroom.

2. CHECK-UP: Imagine that you have a $600.00 balance in your checking account. Write 5 checks, each one for a different amount but none for more than $75.00. Make one deposit for no more than $95.00. Draw the complete record for these transactions, including check number, date, description, payment/deposit, and balance. Set up your record this way:

Check #	Date	Description	Payment	Deposit	Balance

3. PART-TIME: Many young people enjoy working for some extra spending money. List at least ten jobs you could do to earn money outside your own home. What qualifications must you meet for each job? How much would you expect to be paid for each job listed?

4. TAXING: Every day consumers pay extra monies for items purchased in the form of sales tax. Discover which items where you live are NOT taxed. Figure the total cost of the following shopping list at the rate of sales tax in your area.

    1 pkg AA batteries - $1.99   1 birthday card - $1.25
    1 pkg hamburger buns - $.89   1 box band-aids - $2.59
    1 gallon milk - $2.29   2 lb. bag dog food - $3.19
    1 tube toothpaste - $1.89   1 loaf bread - $.89
    1/2 gallon orange juice - $2.79

5. PARTY: Your parents will allow you to invite five classmates to a slumber party to celebrate your birthday. You may spend no more than $35.00 for refreshments and entertainment. How will you spend your money? Include items and cost of each (check prices in local supermarket).

6.   INTEREST WISE: You can use a formula to compute simple interest.

$$i = prt$$

i = interest
p = principal (amount of money borrowed)
r = rate (% at which interest is charged per year)
t = time for which money is borrowed

How much interest will Mrs. Lewis have to pay on a loan of $10,000 at an interest rate of 12% for three years?

$$i = prt \qquad i = 10,000 \times 12 \times 3 \qquad i = \$360.00$$

Find the amount of interest for the following:

p = $500	p = $1500	p = $600
r = 10%	r = 14%	r = 12.5%
t = 1 year	t = 2 years	t = 1/2 year

7.   SMART SHOPPING: One supermarket sells steak at a unit price of $3.89 per pound. Another supermarket sells steak at a unit price of $3.99 per pound. Is the steak at $3.89 per pound necessarily a better buy? Explain with at least two reasons.

Use the foods section of your local newspaper to find the very best buy on the steak of your choice. How much does it cost, and where will you shop? How much will you save?

8.   WANTS AND NEEDS: Prepare a marketing list for your household for a one-week period. Star (*) the items which are absolutely necessary for your family. How many are there? How many items were not starred? Why not? Estimate (using newspaper advertising) the total cost of your shopping list. If the total is more than your family can afford to spend, which items would you leave on the shelves? Why?

THE ABC'S AND THE MEDIA CENTER

The alphabet is a very important design element in the origin, organization, and operation of a library or media center. To help you appreciate the ABC's of your school or community media center and progam, complete one or more of the following tasks:

1. Determine why learning to alphabetize is an important skill for all students to learn. Write down at least ten different examples in the media center where someone had to alphabetize information.
2. Define each of these library-related words for representative letters of the alphabet: abridged, biography, call number, Dewey Decimal Classification System, fiction, index, multi-media, nonfiction, periodicals, reference materials, subject cards, and unabridged.
3. What would happen in a media center if the alphabetical ordering of materials were to disappear? Write a short story about such a situation.
4. Design an interesting alphabet activity or alphabet game to teach younger children about the ABCs.
5. Browse through the media center and locate a fiction or nonfiction book with a "catchy or clever" title for each letter of the alphabet. Determine whether the title gives the reader good information about the content of the book. Rate each book on the connection between title and content in some way

THE CULTURE OF BOOKS

Books can be very useful resources for teaching and learning about different cultures, ethnic groups, historical periods, and geographic locations. Choose one of the following activities to complete using books and/or other resources found in your media center.

ACTIVITY ONE: Pretend you have been invited to travel in outer space and visit a distant planet of the universe. Your challenge is to select no more than 25 fiction and nonfiction books from your school media center that will best describe our culture to this enthusiastic group of aliens. Make a list of these book titles and give a good reason for each selection.

ACTIVITY TWO: Pretend you have been put in charge of preparing a time capsule for the year 2050. Your job is to select a variety of items most commonly found in a school media center that best reflect the lifestyle of today's young adolescent. Make a list of the items for the time capsule and give a good reason for each selection. *(continued next page)*

Item 1:   A piece of media equipment
Item 2:   A periodical
Item 3:   A set of five pages from an encyclopedia
Item 4:   A picture book
Item 5:   A fiction book
Item 6:   A nonfiction book
Item 7:   A video tape
Item 8:   A set of study prints or posters
Item 9:   A map
Item 10: A computer disk

THE MEDIA MEASURES OF SUCCESS

How do you know whether the media center in your school is serving the many diverse needs of its teachers, students, parents, and community members? There are several ways to measure the success of your media center in order to find answers to this question. Work with a group of classmates and complete one or more of these suggested evaluation tasks.

1. Design a set of correlated surveys to use with students, teachers, and parents of your school. Some questions to consider asking on your survey might be:
   How often do you visit the media center?
   What services does the media center provide that you use most often? least often?
   What pleases you most about your media center? least about your media center?
   Make one suggestion for improving your media center.

2. Conduct a series of individual or small group interviews with students, teachers, and parents of your school. Make a list of common questions you would want to ask these people.

3. Schedule a series of observation sessions in your media center to see who is visiting the media center and what activities they are engaged in at the time. Record what you see during these visits and draw some conclusions about what you observe.

4. Prepare a questionnaire to distribute to citizens of your community who do not have children in school but who might want to make use of your media center in some way. What special needs of requests might they have? What special services might you offer to them? Consider such things as:
   Books in braille for those who cannot see well
   Access to computers for those who cannot afford them
   Tape recordings for those who prefer listening to reading
   Special parking places, ramps, chairs for the handicapped

MEDIA METAPHORS

Like Heinz catsup and Baskin Robbins ice cream, books come in 57 varieties and flavors if one considers the diversity of book shapes, sizes, colors, formats, and topics.

Books do, however, have certain things in common that include the following elements:

Start with the Parts

Books come in lots of different shapes, sizes, and colors, but they do have many things in common. For example, most books in the fiction section of the media center have: AN AUTHOR: the person who wrote the book; A COPYRIGHT PAGE: the page either before of after the title page that has the copyright notice and tells the publisher and other important legal information about the book; A COVER: either a hardback or paper outside binding; A DEDICA-TION: the page on which the author dedicates the book to someone as a token of affection; AN ILLUSTRATOR: the person who illustrated the book; A SPINE: the part of the book with the call number on it that you can see when it is on the shelf; A TABLE OF CONTENTS: the page that gives the title of each chapter and the page number on which each begins; A TITLE: the name of the book; A TITLE PAGE: the page of a book that tells the title, author, and illustrator.

Select any 8 books from the fiction section of the media center and look through them to locate the parts listed above. Then design an original title page for a book you would like to write some day. On the back of the title page, write out a special dedication to the person of your choice.

Try comparing the parts of a book with the parts of other interesting objects such as the parts of a flower (roots, stem, leaves, buds, blossoms, etc.) How might they be alike and how might they be different?

Finally, pretend you have been asked to write a "book about books." Outline your plans for this best seller by creating a mock booklet with the following elements: *Title, Book Cover, Title Page, Copyright Page, Dedication Page,* and *Table of Contents.*

Where has this shoe been? Draw a cartoon story about its adventures.

What are all the things you can do with shoes besides wear them on your feet?

How does it feel to be "walked on" all day?

Write four–word sentences. The four words should begin with S–H–O–E.
Example: *S*hould *H*arry *o*perate *e*levators?

Write a story or poem about the time in your life when you were trying to learn to tie your shoes.

Compare/contrast cowboy boots and ballet slippers.

What does it mean to be a shoe–in?

What if shoes could be invisible any time they wanted to be?

Describe the life cycle of a shoe.

List all the materials that shoes are made of.

Do a shoe survey of your family. How many pairs does each member have? How many different colors, styles, conditions (old/new) or values are there? Graph your results.

If shoes could talk, what would a pair from America say to a pair from Japan?

Do you think Americans should ONLY buy shoes manufactured in America? What is your opinion?

Which is more practical — sneakers or boots? Write a debate between the two.

What if wing–tip shoes could fly? Draw a pair. Write a story.

What if it were against the law for adults to wear shoes?

Draw a pair of shoes with at least 25 different details.

If there is a tooth fairy, why isn't there a shoe fairy?

What is the history behind penny loafers?

List all the things shoes CAN'T do.

Compose a Bill of Rights for shoes.

Write a conversation between Michael Jordan's shoes and a basketball.

Design a pair of shoes that would allow you to walk on water.

Estimate the number of shoes in a shoe store at the mall. The next time you visit that store, check your estimation with the manager. How close were you?

Ask your parents, grandparents, and great grandparents to describe the styles of shoes they wore when they were growing up.

Adapted from: Nancy Johnson, *Thinking is the Key: Questioning Makes the Difference* (1992) Pieces of Learning. 1610 Brook Lynn Drive, Beavercreek, OH 45432-1906

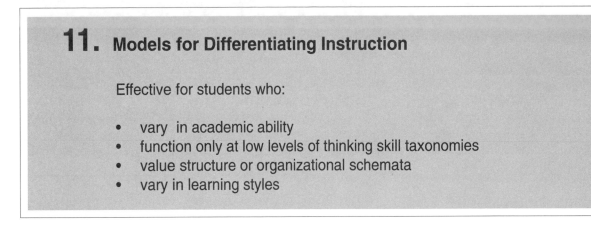

11. Models for Differentiating Instruction

Effective for students who:

- vary in academic ability
- function only at low levels of thinking skill taxonomies
- value structure or organizational schemata
- vary in learning styles

 Traditional models for structuring learning tasks and curricular objectives is another valuable tool for dealing with individual differences in the classroom. There are several options that can be used for this purpose which are:

1. Bloom's Taxonomy of Cognitive Development
2. Williams' Taxonomy of Creative Thinking
3. Gardner's Theory of Multiple Intelligences
4. Krathwohl's Taxonomy of the Affective Domain
5. DeBono's Thinking Hats Model

Teachers should use these models to design worksheets, discussion questions, classroom quizzes/tests, interdisciplinary units, homework, and independent study guides for students. The purpose of these models is to provide teachers with a set of guidelines for developing learning tasks that are both consistent with learning theory and yet flexible enough to allow for individual student differences. Outlines of these five models are included on the following pages complete with sample lesson plans that show applications of how these models can be used in any subject area.

> Refill as often as necessary

BLOOM ACTION VERBS FOR CLASSROOM ACTION

KNOWLEDGE: Knowledge is defined as the remembering of previously learned material. This may involve the recall of a wide range of material, from specific facts to complete theories, but all that is required is the bringing to mind of the appropriate information. Knowledge represents the lowest level of learning outcomes in the cognitive domain.

RELATED ACTION VERBS

Acquire	Follow	Locate	Quote	Reproduce
Choose	directions	Match	Read	Select
Count	Group	Memorize	Recall	State
Define	Identify	Name	Recite	Tabulate
Distinguish	Indicate	Outline	Recognize	Trace
Draw	Know	Pick	Record	Underline
Fill-in	Label	Point	Repeat	Write
Find	List			

COMPREHENSION: Comprehension is defined as the ability to grasp the meaning of material. This may be shown by translating material from one form to another (words to numbers), by interpreting material (explaining or summarizing), and by estimating future trends (predicting consequences or effects). These learning outcomes go one step beyond the simple remembering of material, and represent the lowest level of understanding.

RELATED ACTION VERBS

Account for	Distinquish	Generalize	Paraphrase	Reword
Associate	Draw	Give in	Predict	Rewrite
Change	Estimate	own words	Prepare	Restate
Classify	Expand	Give	Put in	Show
Conclude	Explain	examples	order	Simplify
Compare	Express	Group	Read	Suggest
Contrast	in other	Infer	Rearrange	Summarize
Convert	terms	Illustrate	Recognize	Trace (on
Demonstrate	Extend	Interpolate	Reorder	map or
Describe	Extrapolate	Interpret	Reorganize	chart)
Determine	Fill in	Measure	Represent	Transform
Define	Find	Outline	Retell	Translate
Differentiate				

APPLICATION: Application refers to the ability to use learned material in new and concrete situations. This may include the application of such things as rules, methods, concepts, principles, laws, and theories. Learning outcomes in this area require a higher level of understanding than those under comprehension.

RELATED ACTION VERBS

Apply	Determine	Generalize	Perform	Record
Calculate	(calculate)	Graph	(except in	Relate
Choose	Develop	Illustrate	math or in	Restructure
Classify	Discover	Interpret	public)	Select
Collect	Discuss	Interview	Plan	Show
information	Distinguish	Investigate	Practice	Solve
Complete	between	Keep records	Predict	Track (in
Compute	Employ	Locate	Prepare	develop-
Construct	Estimate	(informa-	Present	ment,
Construct	Examine	tion)	Produce	history,
using	Expand	Make	Prove	process)
Convert	Experiment	Manipulate	(in math)	Transfer
(in math)	Express in a	Model	Put into	Translate
Differenti-	discussion	Modify	action	Use
ate between	Find	Operate	Put to	Utilize
Demonstrate	(implies	Organize	use	
Derive	investigation)	Participate	Put together	

ANALYSIS: Analysis refers to the ability to break down material into its component parts so that its organizational structure may be understood. This may be relationships between parts, and recognition of the organizational principles involved. Learning outcomes here represent a higher intellectual level than comprehension and application because they require an understanding of both the content and the structural form of the material.

RELATED ACTION VERBS

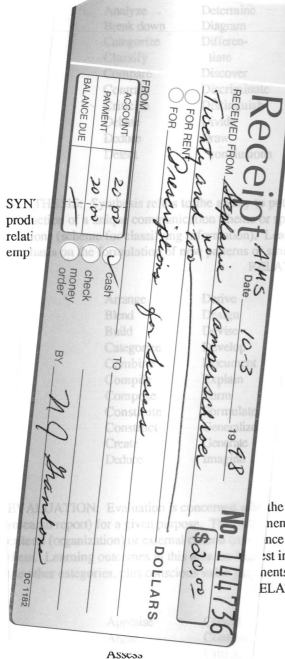

Analyze	Determine	...mine	Make inferences	Search
Break down	Diagram	...mulate	Order	Select
Categorize	Differen-	...m gener-	Outline	Separate
Classify	tiate	...izations	Point out	Simplify
Contrast	Discover	...amine	Put into	Sort
	Discriminate	...oup	(categor-	Subdivide
		...entify	ies)	Survey
Deduce	Draw...	...ustrate	Recognize	Take apart
Defend	...ructions	...fer	Relate	Transform
		...spect		Uncover

SYN... Synthesis re... ...rts together to form a new whole. This may involve the produ... ...ch), a plan of operations (research proposal), or a set of abstract relation... ...ing outcomes in this area stress creative behaviors, with major emph... ...tures.

...ED ACTION VERBS

Integrate	Prescribe	Revise
Invent	Present (an	Rewrite
Make up	original	Specify
Modify	report or	Suppose
Originate	work)	Summarize
Organize	Produce	Synthesize
Perform (in	Propose	Tell
public)	Rearrange	Transmit
Plan	Reconstruct	Write
Predict	Relate	
Prepare	Reorganize	

...the ability to judge the value of material (statement, novel, poem, ...nents are to be based on definite criteria. These may be internal ...nce to the purpose) and the student may determine the criteria given ...st in the cognitive hierarchy because they contain elements of all of ...nents based on clearly defined criteria.

...ELATED ACTION VERBS

	Determine	Interpret	Standardize
	Discriminate	Measure	Summarize
	Distinguish	Rank	Support
Assess	Evaluate	Rate	Test
Award	Critique	Grade	Recommend	Validate
Choose	Decide	Judge	Relate	Verify
Compare	Defend	Justify	Select	
Conclude	Describe			

ARCHITECTURE

KNOWLEDGE: Define the job or role of an architect.

COMPREHENSION: Explain why architecture is more than just a collection of buildings.

APPLICATION: Collect pictures of buildings from magazines, newspapers, photographs, post cards, etc. Then:
  a. Classify all of the buildings according to function. Consider such categories as residential, civic, commercial, spiritual, recreational, etc.
  b. Classify all of the buildings within each category by common visual characteristics.
  c. Determine the list of common characteristics that make up each category of buildings.
  d. Give each category a name or style.

ANALYSIS: Adopt a building in your community and discover its function, style, and architectural elements. Examine the building's form, materials, ornamentation, construction, entrances, window shapes and types, exterior stairs, porches, galleries, or porticos, roof shapes and details, as well as chimneys.

SYNTHESIS: Invent your own architectural style and then make a model or drawing of your building. Combine your building model with others created by members of your class and form a "new" neighborhood.

EVALUATION: Assume you have been asked to prepare a "building tour" of your neighborhood or community for members of your class. Determine what buildings you would have them visit and justify your choice

WILLIAMS' CREATIVE CLUES FOR EFFECTIVE CUES CHART

LEVELS AND LEARNER EXPECTATIONS	TRIGGER WORDS	
FLUENCY is a skill that enables the learner to generate lots of ideas, oodles of related answers, scads of options, or a bunch of choices in a given situation.	How many? one quantity a few	oodles a bunch scads lots
FLEXIBILITY is a skill that enables the learner to change everyday objects to fit a variety of categories by taking detours and varying size, shape, quantities, time limits, requirements, objectives, or dimensions in a given situation.	variety adapt different re-direct	detour alternatives change
ORIGINALITY is a skill that enables the learner to seek the unusual or the unobvious by suggesting clever twists to change content or coming up with clever responses to seek the novel in a given situation.	unusual unique new	clever unobvious novel
ELABORATION is a skill that enables the learner to stretch by expanding, enlarging, enriching or embellishing a list of finds or possibilities so as to build on previous thoughts or ideas in a given situation.	embellish expand upon build embroider	stretch enlarge enrich add on
RISK TAKING is a skill that enables the learner to deal with the unknown by taking chances, experimenting with new ideas, or trying new challenges in a given situation.	dare estimate explore guess	try experiment predict
COMPLEXITY is a skill that enables the learner to create structure in an unstructured setting or to bring a logical order to a given situation.	improve seek alternatives solve	order intricate
CURIOSITY is a skill that enables the learner to follow a hunch, question alternatives, ponder outcomes, and wonder about options in a given situation.	question inquire ask follow a hunch	wonder puzzle ponder
IMAGINATION is a skill that enables the learner to visualize possibilities, build images in one's mind, picture new objects, or reach beyond the limits of the practical in response to a given situation.	reach fantasize visualize	expand wonder dream

Source: Clements, Susan E., Kolbe, Kathy, and Villalpando, E. (1980). *Do-It-Yourself Creative Thinking.* Kolbe Concepts, Inc., 3421 N. 44th Street, Phoenix, AZ 85018.

ARCHITECTURE

FLUENCY: List as many buildings as you can identify in your community that are interesting forms of architecture to you.

FLEXIBILITY: Write down as many reasons as you can think of for preserving historic buildings in a community.

ORIGINALITY: Sketch a picture or write a visual picture of the most unusual and unique building you have seen.

ELABORATION: Expand on this idea: "A man's home is his castle."

RISK TAKING: Determine the most "uninteresting or unappealing" building in your community and write a letter to the editor of your local newspaper telling others why you feel as you do.

COMPLEXITY: Determine what responsibility an architect has to a client or community in refusing to design a building that he/she knows is not practical or not aesthetic.

CURIOSITY: If you had an opportunity to invite an architect to come to school and talk to your class, what would you be curious to know about him/her and his/her work?

IMAGINATION: Imagine you were a chef and were asked to go out shopping and buy things to make a city. What ingredients would you buy and what kinds of places would you need?

MULTIPLE INTELLIGENCES

1.	**VERBAL/LINGUISTIC INTELLIGENCE:** This intelligence focuses on one's ability to use words and language – both written and spoken. This intelligence is dominant in such people as novelists, public speakers, and comedians.
2.	**LOGICAL/MATHEMATICAL INTELLIGENCE:** This intelligence is associated with scientific thinking and deals with inductive/deductive reasoning, numbers, and patterns. This intelligence is dominant in such people as computer programmers, lawyers, and accountants.
3.	**VISUAL/SPATIAL INTELLIGENCE:** This intelligence relies on the sense of sight and the visual arts as well as the ability to form mental images and pictures in the mind. This intelligence is dominant in such people as architects, painters, and draftsmen of industrial design.
4.	**BODY/KINESTHETIC INTELLIGENCE:** This intelligence is related to physical movement and the knowledge/wisdom of the body to express emotion or what is referred to as "learning by doing." This intelligence is dominant in such people as actors, athletes, and inventors.
5.	**MUSICAL/RHYTHMIC INTELLIGENCE:** This intelligence is based on the recognition of tonal patterns including sensitivity to sounds from the environment, the human voice, and musical instruments. This intelligence is dominant in such people as advertising executives, musicians, and composers.
6.	**INTRAPERSONAL INTELLIGENCE:** This intelligence involves the ability to work with others in a group and to communicate, verbally and non-verbally, with other people. This intelligence is dominant in such people as teachers, therapists, and politicians.
7.	**INTERPERSONAL INTELLIGENCE:** This intelligence addresses those who enjoy self-reflection, metacognition, and being in touch with their feelings and spiritual realities. This intelligence is dominant in such people as philosophers, psychiatrists, and counselors.

ARCHITECTURE

VERBAL/LINGUISTIC INTELLIGENCE: Verbally describe a building you know while a partner draws it.

LOGICAL/MATHEMATICAL INTELLIGENCE: Use a Venn diagram to analyze several buildings in your community.

VISUAL/SPATIAL INTELLIGENCE: Construct a visual diagram to show what you think the "home" of the future will be like.

BODY/KINESTHETIC INTELLIGENCE: Create and act out a play in which the characters are various buildings in your neighborhood.

MUSICAL/RHYTHMIC INTELLIGENCE: Analyze the different historical periods in architecture through their music.

INTERPERSONAL INTELLIGENCE: Use a human graph to see where members of your class stand in their appreciation of various buildings in Washington D. C.

INTRAPERSONAL INTELLIGENCE: Discuss: "If I could be any historical building in the world, I would want to be . . . and why.

KRATHWOHL'S TAXONOMY

Affective Goal	Operational Definition
5. *Characterization:* Internalization of a value. Value System is consistent with behavior.	The pupil *voices* his beliefs and AFFIRMS his values/
4. *Organization:* Recognizes pervasive values, determines interrelationships of values, organizes value system.	The pupil *reviews, questions,* and *arranges* his values into an ordered system or plan.
3. *Valuing:* Accepting, preferring, and making a commitment to a value.	The pupil *chooses* a concept or behavior that he believes is worthy.
2. *Responding:* Willingness to respond, motivated, gains satisfaction if responding.	The pupil wants to *discuss* or *explain!*
1. *Receiving:* Pays attention, is aware, takes information into account.	The pupil displays attentiveness: *listens, notices,* and *observes.*

Source: Schurr, S. (1989). *Dynamite in the classroom: A how-to handbook for teachers.* Columbus, OH: National Middle School Association, p. 53.

ARCHITECTURE

RECEIVING LEVEL: Take a walk around your school or your neighborhood and notice the different types of buildings you see.

RESPONDING LEVEL: Write a short paper expressing your satisfaction or dissatisfaction with what you see.

VALUING LEVEL: State your beliefs about what you think is good and bad architecture based on your walk.

ORGANIZING A VALUE SYSTEM LEVEL: Prepare a set of guidelines that you would give an architect who was going to build a new house in the area around your school or neighborhood.

CHARACTERIZING BY A VALUE SYSTEM LEVEL: Declare what you and others could do as citizens in your community to encourage recycling of houses in older neighborhoods.

DeBONO'S THINKING HATS

WHITE HAT THINKING: Someone who wears this hat is a thinker who tries to be neutral and objective in the presentation of information. Neutrality is the key.

RED HAT THINKING: Someone who wears this hat is a thinker who focuses on emotions and feelings as an important part of thinking about information. Feelings are the key.

BLACK HAT THINKING: Someone who wears this hat is a thinker who points out what might be wrong, incorrect, or in error when thinking about information presented. Putting negative elements out in front for others to consider is the key.

YELLOW HAT THINKING: Someone who wears this hat is a thinker who is positive and constructive and concerned with positive assessment just as black hat thinking is concerned with negative assessment. Optimism is the key.

GREEN HAT THINKING: Someone who wears this hat is a thinker who values creative thought and generates new ideas and ways of looking at things. Creativity is the key.

BLUE HAT THINKING: Someone who wears this hat is a thinker who controls and orchestrates the thinking processes of the other hats. The blue hat also gives summaries, overviews, and conclusions in dealing with the information. Control is the key.

ARCHITECTURE

 WHITE HAT: Put on your "white thinking hat" and present information on how "to read a building" to determine its architectural style.

 RED HAT: Put on your "red thinking hat" and express how you feel about selected architectural styles.

 YELLOW HAT: Put on your "yellow thinking hat" and share the positive aspects of several architectural styles.

 GREEN HAT: Put on your "green thinking hat" and suggest ways that various architectural styles could be improved or changed for future construction and function.

 BLACK HAT: Put on your "black thinking hat" and point out what might be incorrect, inconsistent, or incomplete about the ideas presented by the other hat thinkers.

 BLUE HAT: Put on your "blue thinking hat" and summarize the group's thinking about the many different architectural styles under review and discussion.

12. Taking Copying Out of Reporting

Effective for students who are:

- disorganized in note taking
- deficient in gathering information for report writing
- unable to rewrite information from one source to another

Most students still rely on the encyclopedia, whether in print form or on the screen of a computer, as the basic source of information for researching and writing reports. Although the encyclopedia is an invaluable tool, too often students copy entries "word–for–word" from a single encyclopedia source because the information is complete, concise, and well–organized. The wiser students, however, will do the same thing but do so from several sources rather than just one. In short, the work is already done for the students, so why shouldn't they take advantage of it? The following exercises provide the teacher with five optional assignments to help kids use the encyclopedia to spark creative thinking and inquiry rather than convergent thinking and plagiarism.

#1

Encyclopedia task one: Assign students to analyze a wide variety of encyclopedia articles to gain insights as to how different types of information are organized within the framework of the encyclopedia format. For example, most encyclopedia articles include a one–sentence or one–paragraph lead that sums up the subject followed by the main part, or body, that provides the details. In an encyclopedia biography, the paragraphs are usually arranged in chronological order while in articles dealing with places and objects, a more analytical organization is used. An article about a city may be divided into sections about history, commerce, people, arts, economics, and geography. An article about inventions may be organized according to the history of the item, how it works, and how it is used. Encourage students to *copy* the various outlines or formats used in these articles rather than information from the articles themselves. Then ask students to write their own biography or a personal piece on a local event or place according to the established encyclopedia outlines.

Encyclopedia task two: Assign students to select a short article from the encyclopedia that deals with a topic they know something about. After reading it, the student rewrites it supplying additional information from other sources or his/her own experiences showing the limitations of encyclopedic articles as well. For example, if a student writes about skateboarding he/she might add details about safety hints or potential dangers. If a student writes about pet hamsters, he/she might add information from personal observations, experiences, or interviews with hamster owners.

Encyclopedia task three: Assign students to select a topic of interest to them and locate two or three articles on the subject from different sources. They might compare versions from two competing encyclopedias, from an old and a new copyright version of the same encyclopedia, from an encyclopedia written for audiences of two different age levels, or from an encyclopedia and a nonfiction book/video/filmstrip. Students should attempt to analyze the information presented in all versions by asking such questions as: (1) Which facts appear in just one? (2) Which facts appear in both or all? (3) Which facts appear to contradict one another? (4) What appears to account for the discrepancies?

Encyclopedia task four: Assign students to select an encyclopedia article and rewrite a simpler version of it for younger students. Encourage students to make their information statements short and to the point with vocabulary that is manageable for students with limited reading and speaking abilities.

Encyclopedia task five: Assign students to select articles from the encyclopedia and adapt them from one format to another which is not considered to be plagiarism. For example, students might convert the information into a play, a puppet show, a speech, a brochure, a diary, or a nonfiction picture book. The formats of these alternative delivery systems automatically force considerable altercation of the original information because of their unique styles and organizational patterns.

> Refill as often as necessary

13. Gaming and Simulations

Effective for students who:

- prefer hands–on, learning by doing tasks
- exhibit strength in bodily–kinesthetic intelligence
- exhibit strength in interpersonal intelligence
- motivated by interactive experiences

 According to Moore and Serby, authors of the book *Becoming Whole: Learning Through Games*, the use of gaming and simulations in the middle level classroom should be an integral part of the instructional program. According to these experts, games provide the setting for such elements as communication expansion, personality growth, mental stimulation, whole learning, thinking convergently and divergently, decision making, verbal and non–verbal learning, memory development, and dealing with reality. Likewise, Moore and Serby point out that games remove fear, provide fun learning, add interest to skills, activate the mind, encourage attention spans to lengthen, develop organizational skills, develop spatial abilities, increase reasoning, give immediate feedback, reduce stress, and build strategies for life. The following pages provide the teacher with lists and/or descriptions of simple games and simulations that can be used effectively in the classroom.

Reference: Moore, G. B., & Serby, T. (1988). *Becoming whole: Learning through games*. Atlanta: TEE GEE Publishing Company.

Arrange 5 to 10 players around in a circle. Each player has a pencil and a blank piece of paper. The first player writes a sentence across the top of the sheet. The sentence can be content specific (if so directed by the teacher as part of a unit of study) or it can be a sentence on any topic of interest to the writer. The sheet is passed to the second player and he/she reads the sentence and then writes a sentence below it. The second sentence must logically follow the first. The second player folds the sheet so that the first sentence is hidden and only his/her sentence can be seen. This sheet is next passed to the third player who reads the second sentence and writes a third sentence that logically follows. The third player folds the paper so that all sentences but his/hers are hidden, and then passes the sheet to the next player and so on. When all players have written a sentence, the first player reads the complete story or to the group.

Students are divided into two or more teams or groups and each team is separated from a view of the other teams. Each team is given a set of identical construction materials such as paper plates, straws, egg cartons, building sets, plastic utensils/containers, cardboard pieces, scotch tape, etc. Before the simulation begins, a person who will not be involved in this activity constructs a model from the designated materials that is not seen by any team. The teams are then instructed to build a model exactly like the original in twenty minutes. Team members choose roles of runners, builders, or observers and each has definite limitations and assignments. These are as follows:
OBSERVERS can look at the original model and are to give descriptions to the runners. They may NOT come to where they can see what the builders are building.
RUNNERS go between the observers and builders relaying descriptions. They may NOT see the original nor can they help with the building.
BUILDERS listen to the descriptions relayed by the runners and attempt to duplicate the original model. They are the only ones who may touch the building. At the end of the twenty minutes, all building stops. The original model is brought to the building site and comparisons are made. The entire group decides which is the most accurate replica.

Discussion will provide interesting insights into communication, interpretation, and teamwork.

Adapted From: Villalpando, E. (1980). *Simulations.* Kolbe Concepts, Inc., 3421 N. 44th Street, Phoenix, AZ 85018.

Students are divided into groups of five or six members. Each member has a sticky label placed on the forehead telling the others how to treat him/her. They do not see their own labels but can read those of the other participants. Labels might say things such as:

> IGNORE ME
> PRAISE ME
> LISTEN TO ME
> AGREE WITH ME
> INTERRUPT ME
> MAKE FUN OF ME
> CONTRADICT ME
> CLARIFY ME

The group selects a topic to discuss for 5 to 10 minutes and must reach a consensus concerning the topic. During this discussion time members should be treated by others as their labels indicate. When the 5 to 10 minutes discussion/consensus time period is over, assemble all those involved in the simulation and discuss the following:

a. Did you figure out what was on your label?
b. What led you to this conclusion?
c. How did you feel about the way you were being treated?
d. Did some individuals in the group act differently than they usually do?
e. What are some ways we "label" people in real life?
f. Can having a label be a good thing? a bad thing?
g. Do students and teacher label one another?
h. Do ethnic groups label one another?
i. If you felt you had a label you didn't like, what are some ways you could change it?

Adapted From: Villalpando, E. (1980). *Simulations.* Kolbe Concepts, Inc., 3421 N. 44th Street, Phoenix, AZ 85018

Playing a variation of "people search" that is tied to a specific content area can be an excellent way to review for a test or quiz. To do this, teachers should prepare a list of task descriptors related to the subject area and provide each student with a copy of the list. Students then circulate among each other looking for classmates who can successfully perform the tasks. Once a student has been found and has demonstrated his knowledge of the task, he/she signs the appropriate line and continues on in the people search activity. The first person who completes the people search assignment is the winner! Sample tasks in several content areas are suggested on the following page.

Geometry Search: Find someone in our math class who:
1. can explain the difference between parallel lines and perpendicular lines.
   Signature: _____
2. can give the definition of an acute angle, an obtuse angle, and a right angle.
   Signature: _____
3. can recite Pythagoras's Theorem.
   Signature: _____

Rocks and Minerals Search: Find someone in our science class who:
1. can compare and contrast metamorhpic, igneous, and sedimentary rocks.
   Signature: _____
2. can identify five precious gems.
   Signature: _____
3. has performed a scratch test.
   Signature: _____

Poetry Search: Find someone in our English class who:
1. knows the author of *Where the Sidewalk Ends.*
   Signature: _____
2. can create an original metaphor.
   Signature: _____
3. can recite at least four lines from a poem by Robert Frost.
   Signature: _____

Geography Search: Find someone in our Social Studies class who:
1. can list the seven continents.
   Signature: _____
2. can describe the importance of the Panama Canal.
   Signature: _____
3. knows something about the territorial conflicts in the Middle East.
   Signature: _____

This game involves pairing students up and pinning a card that contains information on a common topic on the backs of each student couple . The purpose of the game is to give each pair an opportunity to ask only "yes" and "no" questions to guess what is on their backs and how these two pieces of information are related. For example, in a unit on U.S. Government, one student in a pair might have the words "House of Representatives and Senate" while the other student has the words "Congress." Another pair of students might have the words "Bill of Rights" and "Freedom of Speech" respectively. Still another pair of students might have the words "Power of the President" and "Commander–in–Chief of Armed Services."

Another popular game that can be used as an instructional tool in the classroom is a version of "CONCENTRATION." Important terms or concepts for a given subject area could be listed on one set of cards with their corresponding definitions or applications on a second set of cards. Cards are then placed face down in rows and players take turns trying to find matching pairs.

Give each student a clue card such as the one outlined below. Instruct each student to select an important person, place, thing, event, or concept related to a given unit of study. The student writes out a set of clues related to the theme. The clues should be written in such a way that the most general clues are given first with the more specific clues given last so that there is some mystery and logic to the guessing process. Students are then put in small cooperative learning groups of six and they take turns reading off their clues, one at a time, to the others in the group until the item is guessed correctly.

SAMPLE CLUE CARD ON "Benedict Arnold"

CLUE ONE	I was a brave American soldier.
CLUE TWO	I lived during the time of the Continental Congress.
CLUE THREE	I was friendly to both the Americans and the British.
CLUE FOUR	I was in command of the fort at West Point.
CLUE FIVE	I didn't think my service to the colonies was appreciated or recognized enough.
CLUE SIX	I wanted to open up the entire Hudson Valley to the enemy.
CLUE SEVEN	I earned 6,315 British pounds for my work.
CLUE EIGHT	I escaped to a British warship in the Hudson River.
CLUE NINE	I was made an officer in the British Army.
CLUE TEN	I was convicted by the Americans and hanged as a spy.

Refill as often as necessary

Imperialist Review

Topic

Nineteenth and early twentieth century of Africa focusing on European colonial rule

Objective

Students will define imperialism. They will list at least two European nations that possessed colonies in Africa at one time and name two colonies each for those European nations, using names of present African nations. They will review pertinent information involving African history in preparation for a test or quiz.

Materials

- one 8 ounce (224 g) package of candy, such as M & M's®
- pages 67 and 68, reproduced on index paper or heavy stock
- teacher-created review questions of material relating to the history of Africa, especially the period of European colonial rule
- one small paper cup for each student
- six plastic spoons (or surgical latex gloves)

Preparation

1. Have ready the candy, paper cups, and spoons (or gloves).

2. Before class begins, make copies of the nation/colony cards (page 67 or 68). Cut out the thirty cards provided and give each student a card. Students will assume the identity of either a European nation or an African colony.

3. Have a source of possible review questions from your chapter or unit available.

Procedure

1. Distribute a paper cup containing five pieces of the candy to each student. Emphasize that they are not to handle the treat at this time.

2. Take the stack of nation/colony cards and randomly pass them out, one to a student. Be sure that all six of the European nation cards are distributed, with the rest of the cards being from the African colony group.

Source: Fischer, M. W. (1993). *World history simulations.* Huntington Beach, CA: Teacher Created Materials, Inc. P. 65.

Imperialist Review *(cont.)*

Procedure *(cont.)*

3. Have the students take their cups of candy and arrange themselves into six teams which are formed according to the European nation cards they hold. A team is formed by having all nation card holders whose nations or colonies are linked come together as a group. (For example, card holders of Libya, Somalia, and Italy would be a team.) Some teams, such as the British and French contingents, will be significantly larger than others.

4. Give the card holder of each European nation card a plastic spoon or surgical glove. (Handle candy in this fashion throughout the game.)

5. For this activity, when a student answers a review question correctly, that student (nation or colony) will have another piece of candy added to his/her cup. At the end of the competition, each holder of a European nation card will secure one piece more than half of each of his colonies' holdings of candy. For example, if a colony had four pieces of candy, the European nation would take three pieces; if a colony had six pieces, Europe would take four pieces, etc. Make sure students are apprised of this reward system in advance.

6. Proceed with the review game. Ask questions calling upon the student who first raises his/her hand for the answer. If a student is incorrect, call upon a second player, if possible. If not, drop that question and go onto another, eventually returning to the previous question. End after a specified time limit or question limit is reached.

For Discussion

At the end of the game, discuss the feelings of the students who represented colonies, using the following questions:

- How did it make you feel when you saw your knowledge (resources) benefit another player (nation)?

- Did some of you not play as well as you might have played for yourself?

- As a European "mother country," did you feel it was important for your "colonies" to do well? Why?

Background

Africa was carved into sections by European nations by the second half of the nineteenth century. Africans had little say in what was happening. They furnished labor for their imperialist European masters and endured severely limited political rights and freedoms.

In "Imperialist Review," all but six of the students will be forced by the rules of the game to be in servitude to their "colonial masters" in order to win items (candy) for the masters, knowing that most of their resources will be turned over to their " mother country."

Source: Fischer, M. W. (1993). *World history simulations.* Huntington Beach, CA: Teacher Created Materials, Inc. P. 66.

European Nation/African Colony Cards

Cut out the cards.

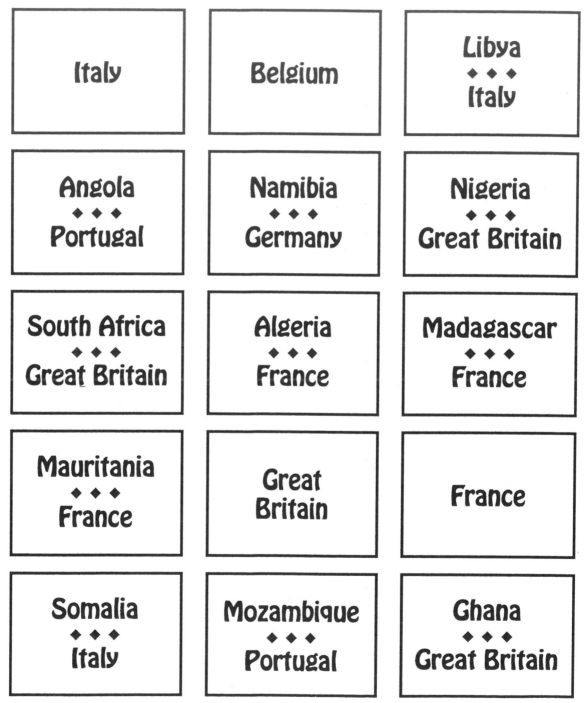

Italy	Belgium	Libya ◆ ◆ ◆ Italy
Angola ◆ ◆ ◆ Portugal	Namibia ◆ ◆ ◆ Germany	Nigeria ◆ ◆ ◆ Great Britain
South Africa ◆ ◆ ◆ Great Britain	Algeria ◆ ◆ ◆ France	Madagascar ◆ ◆ ◆ France
Mauritania ◆ ◆ ◆ France	Great Britain	France
Somalia ◆ ◆ ◆ Italy	Mozambique ◆ ◆ ◆ Portugal	Ghana ◆ ◆ ◆ Great Britain

Source: Fischer, M. W. (1993). *World history simulations*. Huntington Beach, CA: Teacher Created Materials, Inc. P. 67.

European Nation/African Colony Cards *(cont.)*

Cut out the cards.

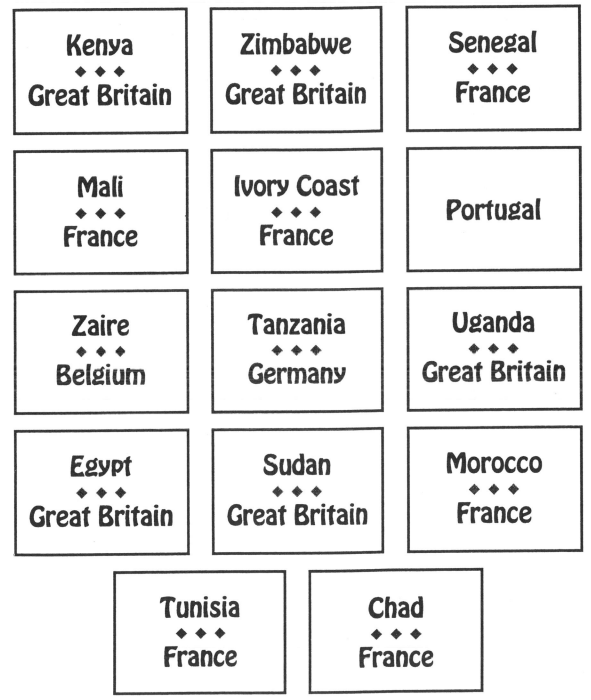

Kenya ◆ ◆ ◆ **Great Britain**	**Zimbabwe** ◆ ◆ ◆ **Great Britain**	**Senegal** ◆ ◆ ◆ **France**
Mali ◆ ◆ ◆ **France**	**Ivory Coast** ◆ ◆ ◆ **France**	**Portugal**
Zaire ◆ ◆ ◆ **Belgium**	**Tanzania** ◆ ◆ ◆ **Germany**	**Uganda** ◆ ◆ ◆ **Great Britain**
Egypt ◆ ◆ ◆ **Great Britain**	**Sudan** ◆ ◆ ◆ **Great Britain**	**Morocco** ◆ ◆ ◆ **France**
Tunisia ◆ ◆ ◆ **France**	**Chad** ◆ ◆ ◆ **France**	

Source: Fischer, M. W. (1993). *World history simulations*. Huntington Beach, CA: Teacher Created Materials, Inc. P. 68.

Pilgrim's Progress

BY KATHY FAGGELLA

It is September 9, 1620. You are a Pilgrim planning a journey from England to America on the *Mayflower*. The voyage will take about seven to eight weeks, and you can only take a limited number of provisions with you. Your task is to look through the following list of items and rank them in order of importance to survival, both on the voyage to America and during the long months ahead. Decide which items are *most important* and number them from 1 to 10. Then decide which items are *least important* and cross them off your list.

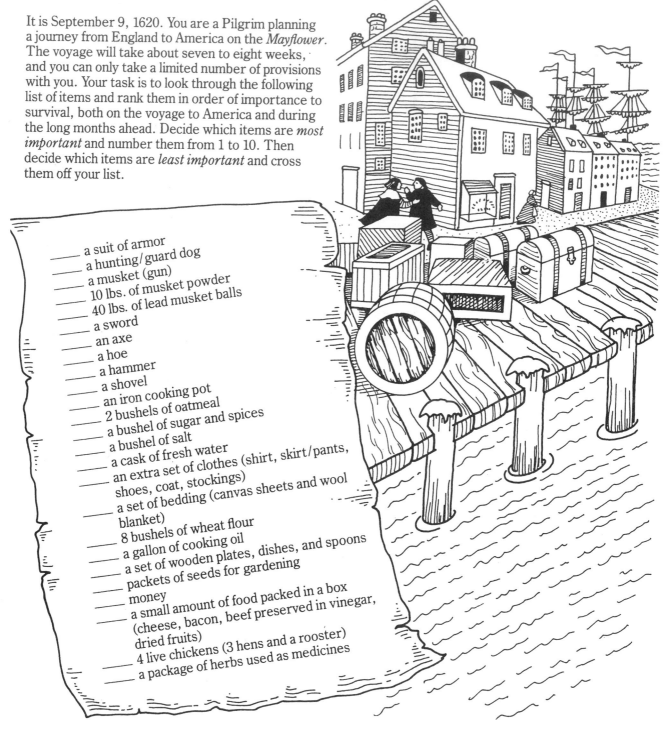

_____ a suit of armor
_____ a hunting/guard dog
_____ a musket (gun)
_____ 10 lbs. of musket powder
_____ 40 lbs. of lead musket balls
_____ a sword
_____ an axe
_____ a hoe
_____ a hammer
_____ a shovel
_____ an iron cooking pot
_____ 2 bushels of oatmeal
_____ a bushel of sugar and spices
_____ a bushel of salt
_____ a cask of fresh water
_____ an extra set of clothes (shirt, skirt/pants, shoes, coat, stockings)
_____ a set of bedding (canvas sheets and wool blanket)
_____ 8 bushels of wheat flour
_____ a gallon of cooking oil
_____ a set of wooden plates, dishes, and spoons
_____ packets of seeds for gardening
_____ money
_____ a small amount of food packed in a box (cheese, bacon, beef preserved in vinegar, dried fruits)
_____ 4 live chickens (3 hens and a rooster)
_____ a package of herbs used as medicines

Source: Faggella, K. (1990, October). Pilgrim's progress. *Instructor Magazine*, 81. Scholastic, Inc. New York. (Reproducible Page).

Trial for Treason!

Work in a group of three or four students.

THE PROBLEM: It is the year 1777. One member of your group has been involved in the fight for independence from Great Britain. He or she has been arrested and transported to London, where he or she will be tried for treason!

If acquitted, he or she will go free.

If found guilty, he or she will hang!

Your group must help this person prepare a defense. The only source material you may use for your defense is Jefferson's Declaration of Independence.

THE PROCEDURE: Work with your group in class.

All the students in a group must prepare the person's defense.

Only one person from a group will speak to the class. The person may speak as the defendant or as the defendant's attorney.

Use group time wisely to prepare a good defense. Select the person to speak who you feel will do the best job. The entire group will receive the same grade, based primarily on the content of the speech given by that one person.

The speaker should expect to talk for approximately three minutes.

THE CONCLUSION: At the end of each presentation, each group must submit to the teacher one sheet of paper with all the names of the group members on it, as well as a brief list of the main points the speaker planned for his or her speech.

After all speeches have been given, the class will vote to determine which speaker was the most powerful and did the best job.

(Prepare well! We hope to avoid any hangings!)

Source: Bourman, A. (1989). *61 cooperative learning activities: Thinking, writing, and speaking skills*. Portland, ME: J. Weston Walch, Publisher. P. 79.

Spending Priorities for a Poor Nation

Work with one partner or in a group of three students.

In very poor, "third-world" nations, governments must constantly look for ways to alleviate poverty. They must spend money on many things, such as:

1. Birth-control education
2. Food, free or inexpensive for the poor
3. Housing, free or inexpensive for the poor
4. National defense
5. Providing jobs for everyone
6. Medical care, free or inexpensive for the poor
7. Primary education
8. Secondary education
9. Colleges and universities
10. Technical education
11. Health education
12. Child-care centers for working parents and for educating parents in proper child care
13. Redistribution of land
14. Intensive literacy campaign
15. Building heavy industry
16. Re-education about outdated or harmful traditions

Discuss how to arrange this list in order of priorities. Where should he government concentrate its spending to improve the country? All items are important, but which should come first, second, and so on? Argue out your differences. Write out and be ready to defend to the class your ordering of the list. Listen to what other groups did with the list.

If you can think of other items to add to the list, do so.

(You can use the same list to argue spending priorities for prosperous nations as well, including our own.)

Source: Bourman, A. (1989). *61 cooperative learning activities: Thinking, writing, and speaking skills.* Portland, ME: J. Weston Walch, Publisher. P. 65.

86

Grammar Pop-Up Cards

Several sets of grammar pop-up cards are provided later in this section. For preparation of these cards, please see pages 7-10.

Parts of a Sentence: Two pop-up sets involve the parts of a sentence. Level A has cards with the words **Subject** and **Predicate**. Instructional wording for this level may vary, but here is one possibility: "You have two cards on your desk. One has the word **Subject** and the other **Predicate**. (Review these concepts, if necessary.) I am going to show you a sentence with a section underlined. If the underlined part is the subject, hold up your card that has the word **Subject** on it. Hold up the card with the word **Predicate** if the underlined part is the predicate. Here is the first sentence. (Example: The young boy crossed the street.) Hold up one of your cards. (Allow time for students to answer.) That's right, the answer is **Predicate**. The next sentence is . . ."

Level B cards contain the items **Simple Subject**, **Simple Predicate**, **Complete Subject**, and **Complete Predicate**. This level may proceed in the same manner as described with Level A.

Types of Nouns: Pop-up cards for this concept contain the items **Common Nouns** and **Proper Nouns**. Here is one possible wording for the activity: "You have two cards on your desk. One has the words **Common Nouns** and the other one **Proper Nouns**. I am going to show you a word that will be either a common noun or a proper noun. The word is written with all capital letters so there will be no clues. If you think it is a common noun, please hold up the card with those two words on it. Do likewise if it is a proper noun. (Allow time for questions.) The first word is *TEXAS*. (Allow time for students to answer.) That's right, Texas. It is a proper noun because it is a specific place. The next word is *MARCH*. I'll bet you need to hear this in a sentence before you can get this one right. Okay: *On March 7 of last year . . .*"

Parts of Speech: Two levels of parts of speech pop-up cards are provided. Level A has **Noun**, **Pronoun**, **Verb**, and **Adjective**. Level B adds **Adverb**, **Preposition**, **Conjunction**, and **Interjection**.

Word Groups: Pop-up cards for this concept contain the items **Sentence**, **Fragment**, and **Run-on Sentence**. Here is one possible wording for the activity: "You have three cards on your desk. One has the word **Sentence**, one **Fragment**, and one **Run-on Sentence**. I am going to read a group of words to you. They will be either a complete sentence, a sentence fragment, or a run-on sentence. (If the sentences are shown, explain that a period will always be placed at the end—even though some will be sentence fragments. This is to eliminate clues for the answer, and it is because those who use sentence fragments in their writing almost always follow them with a period.) Hold up one of your cards to show which you think it is. (Allow time for questions.) The first group is *Early in the morning before the sun rises.* (Allow time for students to answer.) That's right, **Fragment** is the correct answer because it is not a complete sentence. Next is . . ."

Verb Tenses: Pop-up cards for the three verb tenses **Present**, **Past**, and **Future** are provided. Here is one possible wording for the activity: "You have three cards on your desk. One has the word **Present**, one **Past**, and one **Future**. I am going to read a sentence to you. Listen to this

From *Shortcuts for Teaching Language Usage* by Flora Joy (pp. 83-84, 90-100). ©1994. *Good Apple,* Parsippany, NJ. Used by permission of publisher.

sentence to determine if the verb tense is present, past, or future. Hold up one of your cards to show which you think it is. (Allow time for questions.) The first sentence is *The lost little girl screamed for help.* (Allow time for answers.) That's right, **Past** (tense) is the correct answer because it has already happened and it is therefore in the past. Next is . . ."

Types of Sentences: Pop-up cards for the four types of sentences are provided. Here is one possible wording for the activity: "You have four cards on your desk. One has the word **Declarative**, one **Interrogative**, one **Imperative**, and one **Exclamatory**. I am going to read a sentence to you. Listen to this sentence to determine which type it might be. Hold up one of your cards to show which you think it is. (Allow time for questions.) The first sentence is *There's a huge monster standing behind you!* (Allow time for answers.) That's right, **Exclamatory** is the correct answer because of the strong feeling expressed. Next is . . ."

Uses of Nouns or Pronouns: Two levels of pop-up cards for nouns and pronouns are provided. Level A includes **Subject, Direct Object**, and **Object of the Preposition**. Level B adds the **Indirect Object** and the **Subject Complement**. Here is one possible wording for the Level B activity: "There are five cards on your desk. Each one states a use for a noun or pronoun in a sentence. I am going to show you a sentence with a noun or pronoun underlined. Study this sentence to determine the use of that noun or pronoun. Hold up one of your cards to show which you think it is. (Allow time for questions.) The first sentence is *Fred gave me the answer.* (Allow time for answers.) That's right, the pronoun *me* is the indirect object because it tells to whom something is being given—without using the word *to*. The next sentence is . . ."

Sentence Forms: Pop-up cards for four types of sentences are provided. Here is one possible wording for the activity: "You have four cards on your desk. Each one identifies a form of a sentence that we have studied in the past. I am going to read a sentence to you. Listen to this sentence to determine which type it might be. Hold up one of your cards to show which you think it is. (Allow time for questions.) The first sentence is: *My sister sings while my brother plays the piano.* (Allow time for answers.) That's right, **Complex** is the correct answer because it has one main clause that could be a sentence by itself *(my sister sings)* and one clause that could not be a sentence by itself *(while my brother plays the piano)*. The next sentence is . . ."

Sentences or word groups for the above sets of cards may be written on the chalkboard, on sentence strips (for small-group instruction), or on transparency film to be used with the overhead projector. Several starters for each of these categories are provided. An abundance of additional examples may be found in textbooks and workbooks.

From *Shortcuts for Teaching Language Usage* by Flora Joy (pp. 83-84, 90-100). ©1994. *Good Apple,* Parsippany, NJ. Used by permission of publisher.

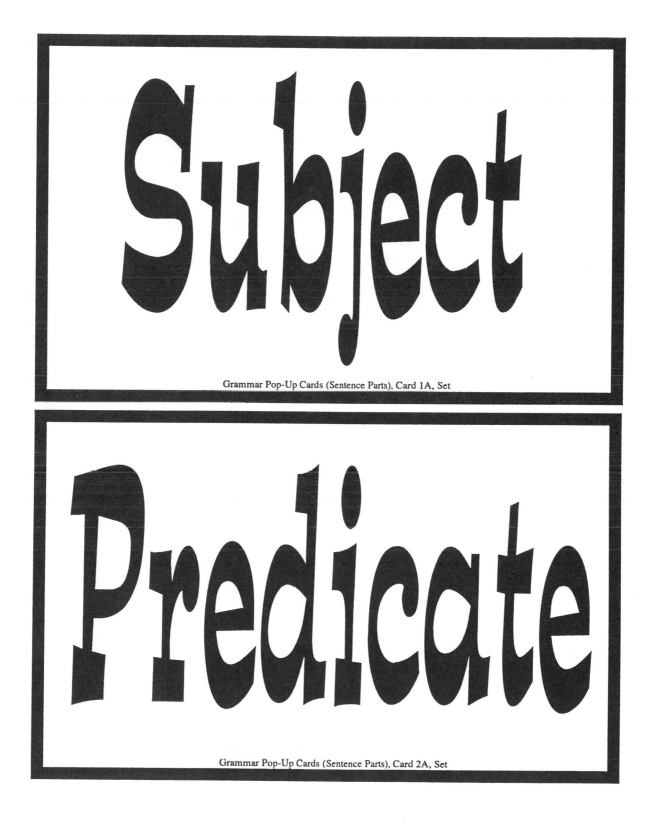

Grammar Pop-Up Cards (Sentence Parts), Card 1A, Set

Grammar Pop-Up Cards (Sentence Parts), Card 2A, Set

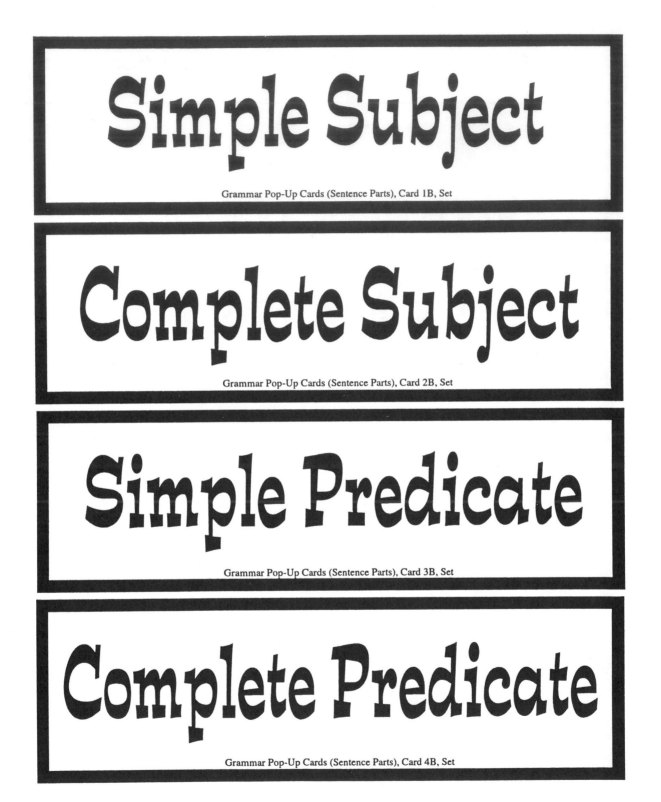

Simple Subject
Grammar Pop-Up Cards (Sentence Parts), Card 1B, Set

Complete Subject
Grammar Pop-Up Cards (Sentence Parts), Card 2B, Set

Simple Predicate
Grammar Pop-Up Cards (Sentence Parts), Card 3B, Set

Complete Predicate
Grammar Pop-Up Cards (Sentence Parts), Card 4B, Set

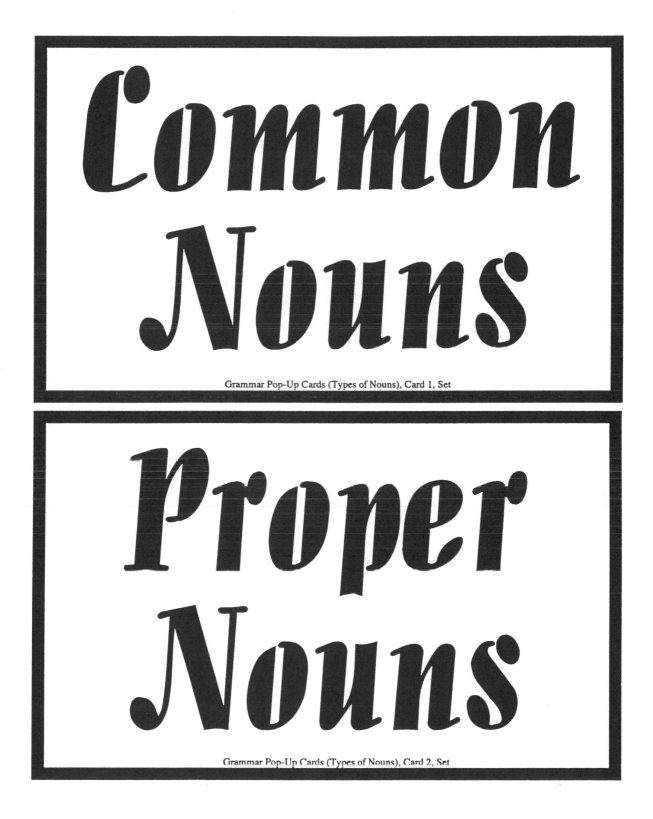

Common Nouns

Grammar Pop-Up Cards (Types of Nouns), Card 1, Set

Proper Nouns

Grammar Pop-Up Cards (Types of Nouns), Card 2, Set

Noun

Grammar Pop-Up Cards (Parts of Speech), Card 1A, Set

Pronoun

Grammar Pop-Up Cards (Parts of Speech), Card 2A, Set

Verb

Grammar Pop-Up Cards (Parts of Speech), Card 3A, Set

Adjective

Grammar Pop-Up Cards (Parts of Speech), Card 4A, Set

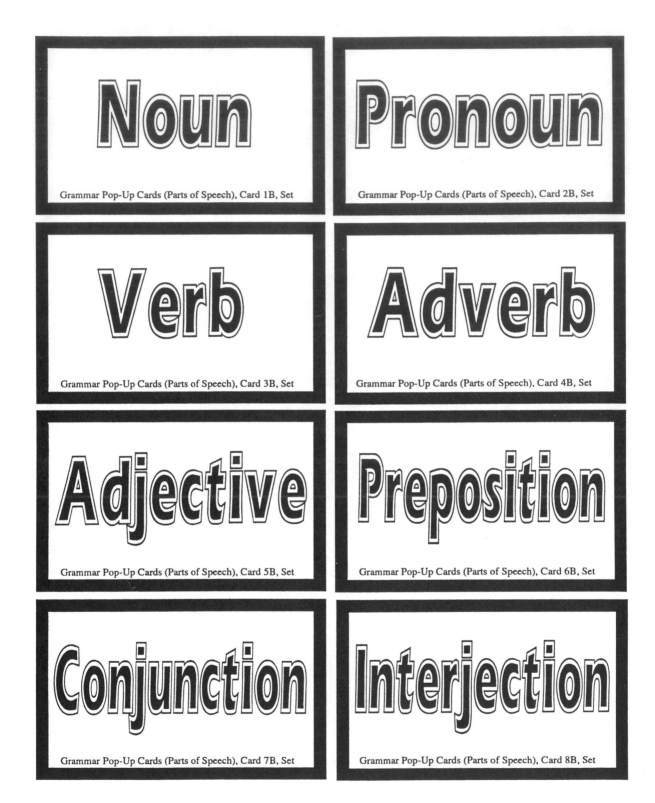

Noun

Grammar Pop-Up Cards (Parts of Speech), Card 1B, Set

Pronoun

Grammar Pop-Up Cards (Parts of Speech), Card 2B, Set

Verb

Grammar Pop-Up Cards (Parts of Speech), Card 3B, Set

Adverb

Grammar Pop-Up Cards (Parts of Speech), Card 4B, Set

Adjective

Grammar Pop-Up Cards (Parts of Speech), Card 5B, Set

Preposition

Grammar Pop-Up Cards (Parts of Speech), Card 6B, Set

Conjunction

Grammar Pop-Up Cards (Parts of Speech), Card 7B, Set

Interjection

Grammar Pop-Up Cards (Parts of Speech), Card 8B, Set

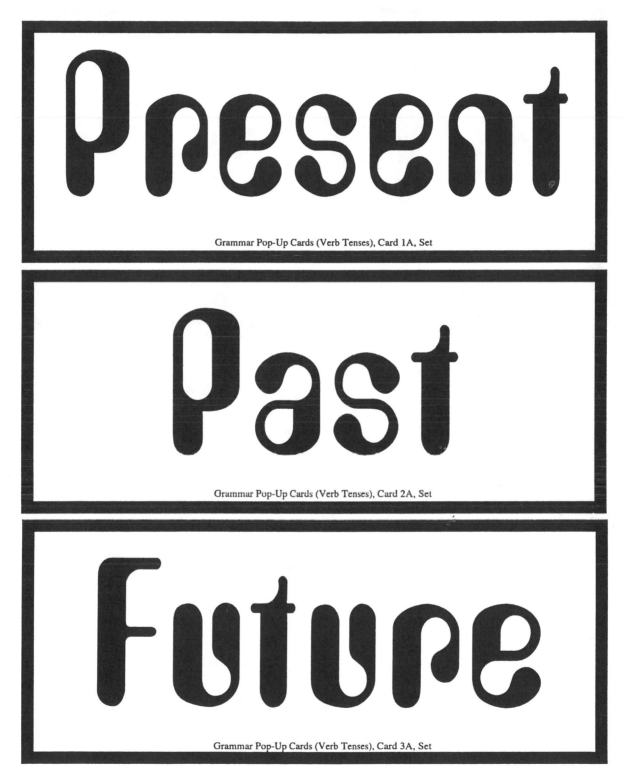

Grammar Pop-Up Cards (Verb Tenses), Card 1A, Set

Grammar Pop-Up Cards (Verb Tenses), Card 2A, Set

Grammar Pop-Up Cards (Verb Tenses), Card 3A, Set

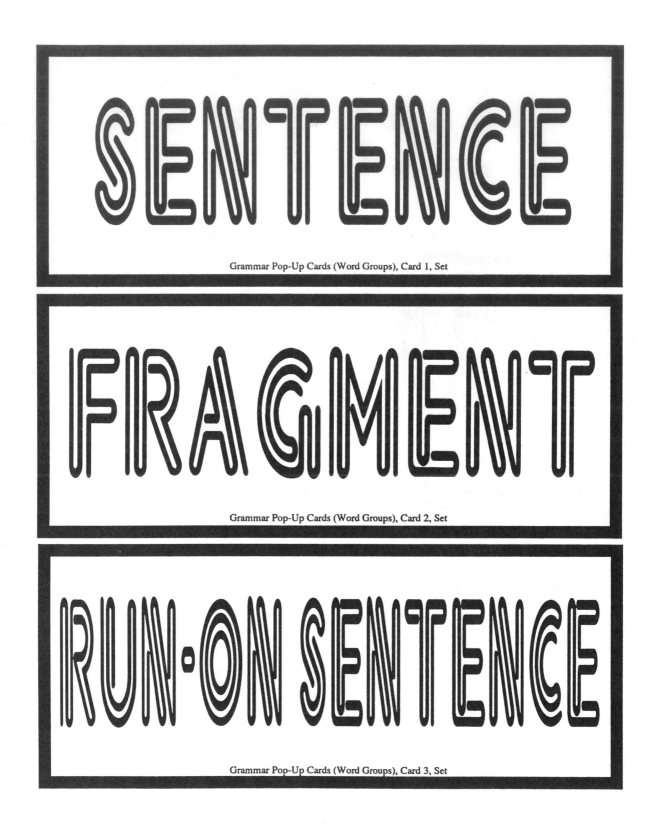

SENTENCE

Grammar Pop-Up Cards (Word Groups), Card 1, Set

FRAGMENT

Grammar Pop-Up Cards (Word Groups), Card 2, Set

RUN-ON SENTENCE

Grammar Pop-Up Cards (Word Groups), Card 3, Set

Declarative

Grammar Pop-Up Cards (Types of Sentences), Card 1, Set

Interrogative

Grammar Pop-Up Cards (Types of Sentences), Card 2, Set

Exclamatory

Grammar Pop-Up Cards (Types of Sentences), Card 3, Set

Imperative

Grammar Pop-Up Cards (Types of Sentences), Card 4, Set

Subject

Grammar Pop-Up Cards (Uses of Nouns or Pronouns), Card 1A, Set

Direct Object

Grammar Pop-Up Cards (Uses of Nouns or Pronouns), Card 2A, Set

Object of the Preposition

Grammar Pop-Up Cards (Uses of Nouns or Pronouns), Card 3A, Set

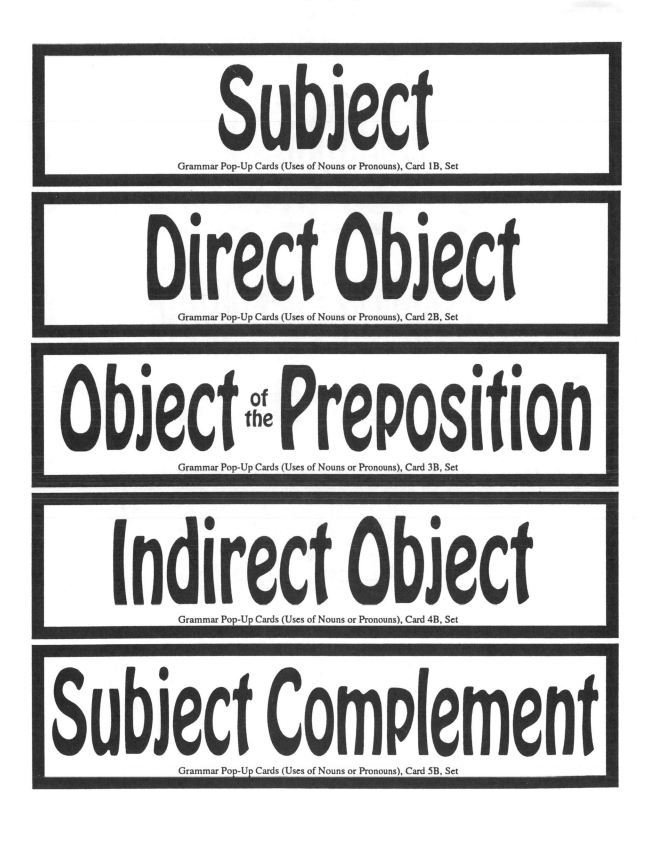

Subject

Grammar Pop-Up Cards (Uses of Nouns or Pronouns), Card 1B, Set

Direct Object

Grammar Pop-Up Cards (Uses of Nouns or Pronouns), Card 2B, Set

Object of the Preposition

Grammar Pop-Up Cards (Uses of Nouns or Pronouns), Card 3B, Set

Indirect Object

Grammar Pop-Up Cards (Uses of Nouns or Pronouns), Card 4B, Set

Subject Complement

Grammar Pop-Up Cards (Uses of Nouns or Pronouns), Card 5B, Set

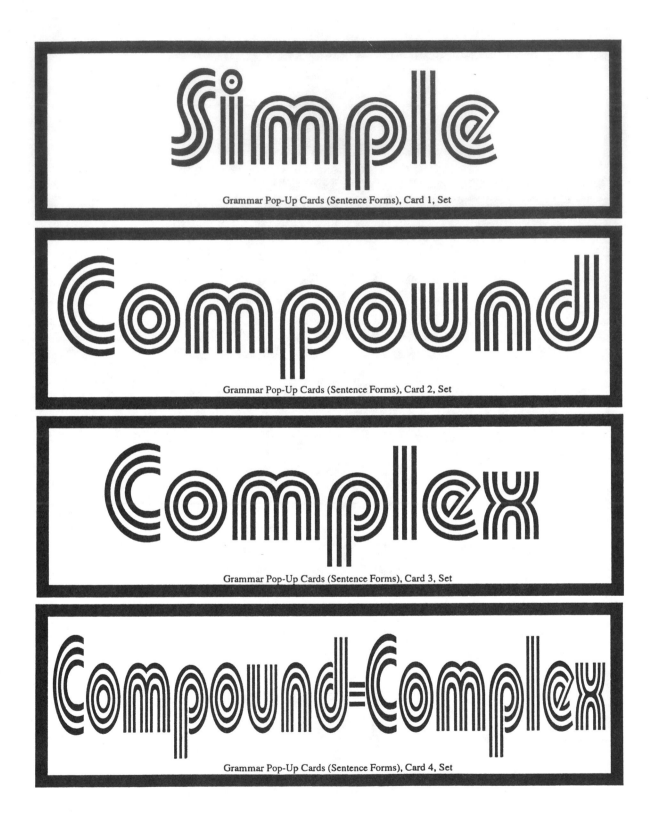

Grammar Pop-Up Cards (Sentence Forms), Card 1, Set

Grammar Pop-Up Cards (Sentence Forms), Card 2, Set

Grammar Pop-Up Cards (Sentence Forms), Card 3, Set

Grammar Pop-Up Cards (Sentence Forms), Card 4, Set

Commercial Games To Use In The Classroom

The following games have been suggested by Gwen Bailey Moore and Todd Serby in their book, *Becoming Whole: Learning Through Games* (1988), for use in the middle level classroom because they promote a wide range of educational and social skills for the early adolescent.

BARGAIN HUNTER: Becoming a smart shopper brings many skills into mental action and reaction. This game is designed to do that. Visual and auditory skills are actually involved along with mathematical concepts. Building strategies and conceptualizing are a big part of your recognizing how to hunt a bargain! Just remember that hunting a bargain doesn't mean that you have to buy it . . . a bargain is never a bargain unless you have a need for the item.

BATTLESHIP: Battleship is a complex game of hide and seek. Not only does it involve deductive reasoning, it creates strategies that are used to find the opponent's hiding ships. Important skills such as eye-hand coordination and fine motor skills are also involved when looking at the game board and determining what actions to take. Other skills involved in this process are visual sorting, visual attention, spatial attention, visual reception, directionality, laterality and color discrimination. This is also an excellent game for auditory reception, auditory attention, motor attention and cross modality. These are all built and strengthened when oral directions are given, and the player must respond with different actions such as putting pegs in the board and saying "hit" or "miss." Battleship is a wonderful game because it builds a foundation for deductive reasoning. The suspense of what is next and being caught escalates as your opponent gets closer and closer to your boat. Battleship builds trust and honesty with other people, but do not let someone sink your ship!

CLUE: Clue is the perfect game for mystery buffs. The object is simple, just find who committed the murder, where it was committed, and with what object. This game is good for providing more abstract thinking as you analyze the incoming information in your quest for the killer. Both visual and auditory skills are included as the information is also important because one must organize all of the clues to make an exact guess. Good luck, working your way through the mansion. Remember that the butler is not even in the game.

LIFE: This game offers us a funny reminder of some common realities of everyday life. Although marriage and having children is forced upon you, you often find yourself motoring along with your family facing one dilemma after another. Life offers extensive practice in coordination of color, hand and eye. Visual skills including perception, memory and discrimination are present. All word attack skills and auditory ones are called for in the game of Life as they are in real life. All attentions are useful in this game including visual, auditory, spatial and motor. Adding and subtracting large numbers provides good mathematical concepts. Directionality runs in circles and so do you before you finally pass your day of reckoning and become a millionaire. What a Life!

Commercial Games To Use In The Classroom (continued)

PASSWORD: Auditory skills come alive in Password as you give synonyms, homonyms, antonyms, analogies and other clues to awaken your partner's word recognition skills. Many skills of association are used along with comprehension and concentration. Word retrieval is a necessity for all players, and it needs to be quick! This is a tremendous game for vocabulary building. It also gives you an on-the-spot interchange with your partner. This is a valuable skill used in all phases of life. "Thinking on your feet" provides children with practice that assists them in becoming less shy and more assertive. This is a sure way to better self-esteem. Many test taking skills are imbedded in Password, and all children need to play. Password is a little difficult for most people because it requires such fast thinking. However, enough practice will allow the fear to diminish. It is time to play!

PICTIONARY: This game may cause a little stress, even for the visual learner. The object is for your teammate to draw a picture and for you to guess what word he is trying to communicate. This game offers a great new twist and an excellent opportunity in developing a sense of suggestiveness from pictures rather than adhering to one's more literal translations of things seen. It even includes the possibility of developing a person's ability to visualize. The game provides many skills that are not found in any other game. For example, drawing pictures to represent words such as citizen, is a skill that we have not found in any other game! It is a great game for provoking and promoting thinking before SAT time rolls around for high school students. This game has all the qualifications for a good time. Your pictures may offer something to think and laugh about for years. Get your crayons ready to roll.

ROOK: Rook is a marvelous card game involving many skills that can be played over a wide range of ages. Through colors, number sequencing and visual discrimination, the cards are sorted, arranged and played. Many of the auditory and sensory skills are present and in action through the interchange of building, calling trumps and playing. The game offers much in mathematical estimation. For example, counting, adding and subtracting are a constant focus. Rook gives the learner a marvelous chance to develop judgement and common sense. Many strategies can be tried and sorted, finally allowing good ones to be selected for use and poor ones to be discarded. Educational and social skills are so prevalent in this game that you will add to your list for a long time. Watch out! The Rook is ready to take you!

Commercial Games To Use In The Classroom (continued)

SCORE FOUR: Score Four is a fun game that can be played with two or more people. Fine motor and eye-hand coordination take the lead in skills for this game as they race with strategy. Every phase of attention settles in quickly or your opponent will stack four balls on a stick before you know it! Perception and spatial awareness become the name of the game as you get further involved in playing. Watching up, down, back and forth, is hard enough, but adding four levels of this keep your eyes jumping! The final wipeout is when your short term memory slips and your opponent sneaks in with a diagonal win. When you would like to see a child's coordination and fine motor skills improve in the writing fingers, nothing is better than Score Four. (It surely is an improvement over poking peas through a hole in the top of a baby food jar!) The quickness of this game adds much interest for children and allows perspective to develop at early ages. It is also pure joy to sit and devise new strategies, keep a straight face and hope to "pull one over" on your opponent!

SENTENCE SCRABBLE FOR JUNIORS: Search and find words, pictures, upper and lower case letters and minute punctuation marks. Look up, down, left and right. Search . . . locate . . . compare . . . match . . . decide and win as you combine your auditory, visual and spatial attentions to complete the sentences in this game. The amount of visual sorting or discrimination is a little overwhelming as the game begins but the difficulty decreases as the game progresses. Visual closure skills aid you in finally inserting each missing part. Hundreds of separate little skills begin to cooperate and coordinate as you attack each word and each sentence. Tracking around this board gives your brain new exercise. Short and long-term memory are in action as you hold and relate information. This game forces you to plan ahead and build strategies in order to become the winner. In every game of Sentence Scrabble for Juniors, you are winning . . . winning a review of skills that may have been otherwise overlooked!

STRATEGO: Stratego, like Chess, requires excellent strategy and tremendous thinking. Before this game even begins, you must set the playing pieces up to suit your mental strategy of play. Short-term memory and long-term memory are both relied upon heavily as one strives to remember the rank of each of his opponents' pieces and where each one is located. Remembering the rank becomes vitally important as each piece is revealed in play. This game is a great build-up for higher thinking strategies and manipulation. Don't get blown away while stepping on a land mine!

14. Leading Effective Discussions

Effective for students who:

- are auditory learners
- exhibit strength in the linguistic intelligence
- exhibit strength in the interpersonal intelligence
- enjoy "learning by doing" activities

 Classroom discussions are important in the middle level classroom for several reasons. (1) they provide the teacher with feedback about student learning, (2) they lend themselves to higher order thinking skills, (3) they help students develop interests and values as well as to change attitudes, (4) they allow students to become more active participants in their learning, and (5) they enable students to hear and offer alternative points of view and to explore complex issues. On the other hand, there are some disadvantages to discussion sessions which include: (1) difficulty in getting student participation as they may be threatening to students because of peer pressure to excel; (2) time consuming to conduct; (3) not always well suited to covering significant amounts of content; (4) require more forethought and planning on the part of the teacher than lecture; and (5) provide teacher with less control than other means of instruction. It should be noted, however, that students are more likely to participate successfully in discussions if the instructor:

- carefully plans and prepares for discussion topics,
- deals with experiences common to students,
- encourages and recognizes students' contributions,
- provides regular summaries and conclusions,
- uses divergent questions,
- challenges students without threatening them,
- moves about the room rather than standing in one place,
- provides students with short, informal in–class writing activities that can be used productively to focus student attention and stimulate student thought initially on a discussion topic as well as brief, written summaries or reactions to the discussion's main points.

According to Hyman (1987), there are five common types of discussions that can be used effectively in the middle level classroom.

1. Explaining discussions that analyze the causes, reasons, procedures, or methods of what has occurred.

2. Problem solving discussions that seek to address a conflict or problem facing the group or the larger community outside the classroom.

3. Briefing discussions that reflect on the facts, meanings, and implications of a shared activity such as a field trip, viedotape, or guest speaker.

4. Predicting discussions that predict the probable consequences of a given situation, condition, or policy.

5. Policy deciding discussions that set policy on how the group should act or recommends policy for the larger community outside the classroom.

Source: Hyman, R. T. (1987). Discussion strategies and tactics. In W. W. Wilen (Ed.). *Questions,questioning techniques, and effective teaching.* Washington, D.C.: National Education Association.

Refill as often as necessary

15. Personality Profiles

Effective for students who:

- exhibit strength in the intrapersonal intelligence
- enjoy data collecting about themselves
- perform best when teaching is matched to their learning styles

 Students enjoy finding out "who they are" and "what makes them tick." Administering a wide variety of informal learning style inventories and/or personality checklists can become excellent tools for helping students identify their strengths and their weaknesses. They can also become effective springboards for dialogue among students and between students and teachers. The following pages contain a number of sample inventories and checklists that could be used for this purpose.

Refill as often as necessary

Your Colorful Personality

Colors often remind people of different qualities. Maybe red makes you think of anger, or blue makes you think of peace. Some people believe that your favorite color says something about your personality.

PART I: Write the name of your favorite color here: _____

Write one thing you think your favorite color says about you:

_____

Match the colors in the left-hand column with the personality traits described in the right-hand column.

COLORS	PERSONALITY TRAITS
RED	A. Patient and persistent. Poised and dignified. A rational decision maker.
GREEN	B. Intellectual and spiritual. Wise and high-minded. Inventive and creative.
ORANGE	C. Tradition and authority are important. A solid citizen, admired by many.
BLUE	D. Courageous, energetic, enthusiastic, restless. Passionate and impulsive!
YELLOW	E. Sensitive and refined. High standards. Has a devoted circle of close friends.
PURPLE	F. Warm nature. Filled with the joy of life. Inspires others to reach their highest potential. Popular; a leader.

PART II: How does each of these colors make you feel? What does it make you think of? Write the first answers that come to mind.

RED _____

_____

_____

ORANGE _____

_____

YELLOW _____

_____

GREEN _____

_____

_____

BLUE _____

_____

_____

PURPLE _____

_____

PART III: Color each of the shapes below with one of these six colors: red, orange, yellow, green, blue, purple. (Decide which shape "looks" yellow, blue, etc., to you.)

From *Psychology for Kids: 40 Fun Tests That Help You Learn About Yourself* by Jonni Kincher, copyright © 1995. Reprinted with permission of Free Spirit Publishing Inc., Minneapolis, Minn; (800) 735-7323. ALL RIGHTS RESERVED.

What's Your STYLE?

PART I: Most people match up the colors and personality traits like this:

Red: D
Green: C
Orange: F
Blue: A
Yellow: B
Purple: E

What's your favorite color? Do the personality traits for that color fit you? If they don't, then Part I of this PSI isn't true for you. That's okay. Color can still tell you about your personal style.

PART II: Color can make us feel certain ways. For example, orange is believed to make people hungry. (That's why so many fast-food restaurants are painted orange inside.) Bubblegum pink is believed to calm people down. (It has been used in prisons.)

There's a scientific explanation for how color affects our feelings. Each color has a particular wavelength. When it strikes the color-sensitive cones at the back of the eye, the cells fire, sending nerve signals to the brain. This may release certain brain chemicals which determine our moods.

There's no right or wrong way to respond to color. Orange may make you feel hungry — or it may make you feel too nervous to eat. The way you feel about color is part of your personal style.

> "What a joyous thing is color! How influenced we all are by it, even if we are unconscious of how our sense of restfulness has been brought about."
>
> — *Elsie De Wolfe, actress and writer*

PART III: Ask a friend or family member to do this coloring exercise, too. Compare your answers. How are they alike? How are they different? Remember that there's no right or wrong way to feel about color.

Find Out MORE

- What's your favorite color for each of these things?

  winter sweater

  summer sweater

  your car
  (pretend you have one)

  your parents' car

  your house

  your room

  your school

  your bike

  your pet

  your favorite jacket

- Experiment with color in your own room. For one week, put a colored sheet over your window, or a colored shade on a lamp. At the end of the week, write about how it felt to live with that color. Try different colors until you find one you really like.

- What was your favorite color last year?

■

Color Response Survey

Find out how other people respond to color. Take a survey!

Invite six people to participate in your survey. Use the chart on the next page. Write their names in the boxes in the left-hand column. Then ask them how they feel about each of the colors in the other six columns. Record their responses.

■

Color Response Survey

Name of Person	Black	White	Red	Blue	Yellow	Green

How Impulsive Are You?

Are you the sort of person who does things on the spur of the moment?

1. Are you easily bored by routine? ☐
2. Do you think that too much planning takes all the fun out of life? ☐
3. Do you usually make up your mind quickly? ☐
4. Do you ever act first and regret later? ☐
5. Do you buy clothes on impulse? ☐
6. Do you buy food on impulse? ☐
7. Do you ever buy things you don't really want? ☐
8. Do you ever buy clothes you never want? ☐
9. Do you ever buy books you never read? ☐
10. Do you ever accept invitations that you later regret? ☐
11. Do you ever get yourself into a mess by acting before thinking? ☐
12. Do you make last minute holiday arrangements? ☐
13. Do you usually sleep on things before making major decisions? ☐
14. Do you have a tendency to sum people up after a first meeting? ☐
15. Do you ever organize spur-of-the-moment parties? ☐

CHECK YOUR SCORE

1.	yes	1	no	0
2.	yes	1	no	0
3.	yes	1	no	0
4.	yes	1	no	0
5.	yes	1	no	0
6.	yes	1	no	0
7.	yes	1	no	0
8.	yes	1	no	0
9.	yes	1	no	0
10.	yes	1	no	0
11.	yes	1	no	0
12.	yes	1	no	0
13.	yes	1	no	0
14.	yes	1	no	0
15.	yes	1	no	0

Total =

If you scored 10 or more, you almost certainly are the type of individual who jumps in where angels fear to tread. You have a tendency to do things first and think about them later. That means that you're often in trouble of one sort or another. On the other hand, it does mean that life is rarely dull.

If you scored between 4 and 9, you do have occasional irresistable impulses, but much of the time you manage to control your impulses.

If you scored 3 or less, you are far too sensible to submit to sudden impulses. You might feel like doing things on the spur of the moment, but you're usually far too sensible to succumb to such temptations.

Source: Coleman, V. (1988). *Know yourself: 940 questions that uncover the real you!* New York: Fawcett Crest. Pp. 100-102.

GUIDE TO OBSERVABLE LEARNING STYLES

Observable behavior is a reliable indication of learning style. Observation helps to confirm data from student self– evaluation and/or other diagnostic measures. Remember that many young teens tend to be quite energetic. A kinesthetic style of learning for them may be an adolescent phase, valid for the present. It may be less a part of their style as they move into adulthood.

Students do not have to exhibit all of the traits in one pattern to exemplify that style. A preponderance of traits, or a few that are intense, may be enough to signify learning strength.

Visual Student

_____ thinks in pictures, visualizes details
_____ is distracted by clutter or movement
_____ can plan in advance; writes thoughts down
_____ states or doodles or finds something to look at when inactive
_____ is often unaware of sounds
_____ remembers by writing things down
_____ likes order in appearance, notebook, locker, desk
_____ may repress emotion, cry easily, or show emotion through facial expression
_____ tends to be a good speller
_____ learns by reading or watching demonstrations

Auditory Student

_____ enjoys listening, but cannot wait to talk
_____ is easily distracted by sounds
_____ reads aloud or subvocalizes
_____ talks problems out
_____ remembers stories and directions after hearing them
_____ hums, talks to self or others
_____ enjoys music more than visual arts
_____ expresses displeasure by "blowing off steam" but calms down quickly
_____ remembers by auditory repetition and saying it
_____ may perform rote memory task well if "sun" to a tune

Kinesthetic Student

_____ drums fingers, taps toes, or asks to leave room frequently
_____ gestures when speaking
_____ is not attentive to visual or auditory presentations
_____ tends to be impulsive
_____ selects options with the greatest physical activity
_____ reflects emotion through body: stamps, pounds, jumps, hits, hugs

_____ pushes hard on pencil, breaks point easily
_____ learns by trying things out: touches and manipulates
_____ tends to have disheveled appearance because of activity
_____ likes sports and games with movement

Left–Brain Learner

_____ responds well to verbal information and explanations
_____ prefers to talk or write
_____ is interested in reward
_____ tends to be reflective, analytical
_____ likes ordered information: logical, sequential, systematic
_____ relies on language in thinking and remembering
_____ likes multiple choice items on tests
_____ solves problems by logical analysis and systematic solutions
_____ is conscious of time, like schedules
_____ can logically explain answers to math (or other) problems

Right–Brain Learner

_____ likes open–ended information
_____ responds well to demonstrations or symbolic instructions
_____ relies on images in thinking and remembering
_____ has difficulty with simultaneous number and word concepts
_____ likes to draw or manipulate objects
_____ has little sense of time; dislikes schedules
_____ prefers essay questions
_____ solves problems with intuition, playing hunches
_____ looks at the whole, rather than details
_____ often knows an answer but may not be able to explain why

16. Questions That Count

Effective for students who:

- enjoy the challenge of creative and critical thinking tasks
- require practice in higher order thinking skills
- need opportunities to speak in small/large groups

 A teacher's willingness to use questioning techniques in a variety of different contexts and according to a taxonomy of higher order thinking skills is important in helping students develop the ability to reason. According to experts (Gall, 1973) a teacher can tell whether student responses are of quality or not by using these seven criteria:

Clarity: The student responds in clear English without hesitation, failing to finish,or confusing his/her thoughts.

Accuracy: The answer contains no factual errors and is based on correct information.

Appropriateness: The student answers the question that was asked and doesn't talk around it."

Specificity: The student gives reasons, facts, or examples to support his/her statement,or he/she explains the criteria or assumptions on which he/she bases his/her opinion.

Support: The student gives reasons, facts, or examples to support his/her statement,or he/she explains the criteria or assumptions on which he/she bases his/her opinion.

Complexity: The student's answer shows that he/she is aware that there are many ways of looking at the problem being discussed, and that he/she must consider before a valid judgment can be reached.

Originality: The learner draws upon current knoweldge and past experience to create or discover ideas that are new.

Source: Gall, M. D. (1973, February). *What effects do teachers' questions have on students?* Paper presented at the Annual Meeting of the American Educational Research Association, New Orleans.

Teachers can find the Question Outline that follows helpful in forming a variety of questions in a diversity of contexts. Teachers might also find Riegle's Question Classification System an excellent tool for structuring their questioning tactics during written or oral activities.

Refill as often as necessary

QUESTION OUTLINE

Quantity Questions:
1. List all of the _____.
2. List as many _____ as you can think of.
3. How many ways can you come up with to _____?

Reorganization Questions:
1. What would happen if _____ were true?
2. Suppose _____ (happened), what would be the consequences?
3. What would happen if there were no _____?

Supposition Question:
1. Suppose you could have anything you wanted in working on this. What ideas could you produce if this were true?
2. You can have all of the _____ in the world. How could you use it to_____?
3. You have been given the power to _____. How will you use it?

Viewpoint Questions:
1. How would this look to a _____?
2. What would a _____ mean from the viewpoint of a _____?
3. How would _____ view this?

Involvement Questions:
1. How would you feel if your were _____?
2. If you were _____, how would you (see, taste, smell, feel)?
3. You are a _____. Describe how it feels.

Forced Association Questions:
1. How is _____ like _____?
2. Get ideas from _____ to improve _____.
3. I only know about _____. Explain _____ to me.

Main Idea:
1. In your own words, what is the most important idea in this *sentence* (paragraph, picture, selection)?
2. What is the topic sentence of this paragraph?
3. What would be a good headline or title for this paragraph?
4. Which of the two titles I gave you (supply two) would be the better headline?

QUESTION OUTLINE (continued)

General - Specific:

Give students a general statement from a story or book they have read. Have them find information in the story to support or refute the statement.

Example: Jerry was always getting into trouble.

Possible Responses:

1.   Jerry's mother became angry when he tracked up her newly waxed floor.
2.   Jerry's teacher became upset when he pulled a little girl's hair.

Fact or Opinion:

1.   Select a series of statements from a selection. Ask students to tell whether each is fact or opinion and why they classified it as such.
2.   What is the main point of the author's argument? Does he use fact or opinion to support his position? Cite examples from the selection to prove your answer.

Smiles, Metaphors, Figures of Speech:

1.   In the sentence what does the phrase _____ mean?
2.   Can you substitute something else to convey the same meaning?
3.   Do the words in the *simile* (metaphor, figure of speech) mean the same when they are used together this way as they do when each is used separately?

Summarizing:

The main objectice here is for the student to express clearly and concisely what a given selection or portion of a selection is about. Questions might include:

1.   Can you tell in one sentence what this whole page is about?
2.   Can you tell in 2-3 sentences what the whole story (book) is about?
3.   Can you tell in one sentence what the whole story is about? (Here you're asking the student to state the theme so the sentence should be complete enough for the purpose.)

Subordinate Ideas:

1.   What facts are given to show that _____?
2.   What sentence answers the following question?
3.   What details support the *main* idea?

Roots, Prefixes, Suffixes:

1.   What is the meaning of _____ in this sentence?
2.   Can you give the meaning of this word without the _____ (prefix, suffix)?
3.   What word could you substitute for _____?
4.   How does the meaning of the sentence change if we eliminate the _____ (prefix, suffix)?

QUESTION OUTLINE (continued)

Classification of Words and Phrases:

Have children suggest a list of words or phrases from a story or book they have read. Have them classify them by one or more of the following:

1. Meaning
2. Function
3. Number of syllables
4. Vowel sounds
5. Other (student suggested and teacher approved)

Cause-Effect Relationships

1. Why did _____?
2. What would happen if _____?
3. What happened because _____ did _____?

Note: Whenever possible, develop the concept of multiple causation.

Key Qualifying Words:

A key qualifying word is one which controls the meaning of a sentence. For example, in the sentence, *Horace fell in the **deep** water,* "deep" is a key qualifying word.

1. What is the meaning of _____ in that sentence?
2. How would it change the meaning if we substituted _____ (supply word) for this word?
3. Can you substitute a word for _____ that gives the sentence approximately the same meaning?
4. Would the sentence make sense if we omitted the qualifying word? Would it meaning change? How does the qualifying word emphasize the sentence meaning?

Analogy:

When a reading selection contains an analogy, ask students to state it. Use questions such as:

1. How does the author describe _____ on page _____?
2. What did the author mean when he said _____ was like _____?
3. Could you say this in another way that would mean approximately the same thing?

Construct A Diagram From Printed Information:

When a reading selection describes a location, have students construct a simple drawing to show how people and places relate to each other.

QUESTION OUTLINE (continued)

Context:

1. What is the meaning of _____ in this particular sentence?
2. Can you substitute another word for _____ in that sentence without changing the meaning?
3. Do you know some other meanings for this word (phrase)?
4. What word means the opposite of _____?
5. What new meaning can you learn for _____?

Drawing Conclusions:

1. Stop at a certain point in the story and ask, "What do you think will happen next?"
2. Based on this story, what kind of person do you think _____ was?
3. How do you think this story will end?

Author's Purpose:

1. Why do you think the author wrote this story (book)?
2. What do you think the author was trying to prove when he wrote this?
3. How do you think the author wanted you to feel as you read this?

RIEGLE'S QUESTION CLASSIFICATION SYSTEM

I. *Empirical:* Questions about the world and our experiences of it.
- A. *Causal:* Questions about the cause of something.
  - Why did the pond freeze?
  - What caused World War I?
- B. *Teleological:* Questions about someone's purpose, aim, or goal.
  - Why did the President of the U.S. visit China?
  - Why did our athletes prefer Atlanta as the site of the 1995 Summer Olympics?
- C. *Functional:* Questions about something's function.
  - Why does the liver secrete bile?
  - What is the function of the pancreas?
- D. *Non-Normative Judgment:* Requests for an estimate, prediction, ranking, or grading, but not of value judgments.
  - How far is the green?
  - Who will win the election?
  - Is the second note higher or lower than the first?
- E. *Descriptive:* Requests for descriptions.
  1. Requests for properties or characteristics.
     - What color is it?
     - What are the properties of iron?
  2. Requests for examples.
     - What are some examples of homonyms?
     - Give me a substance that dissolves in water.
  3. Requests for classifications.
     - Is NaOH an organic or inorganic compound?
     - What class of animals does the cat belong to?
  4. Requests for labels or names.
     - Who is the President of France?
     - Which part of the brain is the lowest?
  5. Requests for summaries.
     - Summarize chapter three.
     - What were the major points of this book?
  6. Requests for reviews.
     - What have we said so far?
     - What did the author say about ecology?
  7. Requests for procedures or processes.
     - How is sulphur mined?
     - How did you get the answer to this problem?

Source: Riegle, R. P. (1976). Classifying classroom questions. In K. A. Strike (Ed.) *Philosophy of education 1976.* Urbana, IL: Philosophy of Education Society.

RIEGLE'S QUESTION CLASSIFICATION SYSTEM (continued)

8. Requests for chronological sequences.
> List in chronological order the events leading up to World War I.
> What sequence of events preceded Coolidge becoming President?

9. Requests for relationships
> What is the relationship between the Big Dipper and the North Star?
> How is spelling ability related to reading ability?

10. Requests for comparisons.
> Compare Alabama to Auburn.
> What do these words have in common?

11. Requests for contrasts.
> Contrast materialism with idealism.
> What is the difference between organic and inorganic compounds?

II. *Analytic:* Questions about the relationships between verbal, logical, or mathematical symbols.

   A. *Linguistic:* Requests for definitions or the relationship between words.
   > Define "placid."
   > What does "ambiguous" mean?

   B. *Logical:* Requests for the laws of logic or the relationship between logical symbols.
   > Why is this argument invalid?
   > Does that conclusion follow?

   C. *Mathematical:* Requests for the laws of mathematics or the relationship between mathematical symbols.
   > What is 6×7?
   > Why does angle A plus angle B equal 180 degrees?

III. *Normative Judgment:* Requests for evaluations, obligatory judgments, or justifications.
> Was Gerald Ford a good president?
> Should *Schindler's List* be banned from the school's curriculum?

Source: Riegle, R. P. (1976). Classifying classroom questions. In K. A. Strike (Ed.) *Philosophy of education 1976*. Urbana, IL: Philosophy of Education Society.

RIEGLE'S QUESTION CLASSIFICATION SYSTEM (continued)

IV.   *Preference:* Questions about likes and dislikes.
        Do you like ice cream?
        Don't you like coming to school?

V.   *Metaphysical:* Questions about supernatural beings, events, etc., which have no agreed upon method for arriving at an answer.
        Is the glass half full or half empty?
        Why is there something rather than nothing?

Source: Riegle, R. P. (1976). Classifying classroom questions. In K. A. Strike (Ed.) *Philosophy of education 1976.* Urbana, IL: Philosophy of Education Society.

118

17. The Magic of Numbers

Effective for students who:

- lack motivation for traditional math
- exhibit strength in logical mathematical intelligence
- enjoy logic puzzles, brainteasers, and optical illusions
- are good at spatial relationships

The following set of mathematical challenges are designed to supplement the traditional math program in order to motivate students who are either bored with many textbook math lessons or are not completing these lessons successfully. They provide students with alternative ways to acquire and apply mathematical principles in new and different ways. These activities can be designated as part of learning station experiences, as part of cooperative learning group tasks, as part of homework assignments, or as part of independent study projects.

Some of these math ideas are outlined below while others follow as reproducible pages.

Math challenge one: Engage students in one or more of the following general mathematical tasks to "tease their minds" and "tickle their imaginations" when it comes to numbers:

a. Research number superstitions and proverbs such as: "13 is considered an unlucky number while 7 and 11 are considered lucky numbers." Proverbs include such number references as: "A stitch in time saves nine" or "A bird in hand is worth two in a bush." Survey adults in your school and community to determine their lucky or unlucky numbers and their understanding of proverb origins.
b. Describe how meteorologists work with numbers in their field.
c. Summarize the importance of numbers in the stock market.
d. Experiment with secret codes based on numbers. Write math messages, math codes, and math riddles to one another.
e. Research to find out more about Egyptian, Greek, and Roman numeral systems.

Math challenge two: Locate a book on optical illusions and try to figure out the logic behind these exciting diagrams. Four of these optical illusions are included here for you to figure out.

I
I ove
Paris in the
the
Springtime

Eyeglasses   Dumbell

Which line is longer?

What is this?

Is this a perfect square?

Solutions: I love Paris in *the the* springtime; same length; west; yes.

Source: *More Illusions and Visual Oddities: 52+ Visual Illusions on Playing Cards.* (1987). Hempstead, NY: Y and B Associates, Inc.

Math challenge three: Integrating math with social studies or science is always an interesting way to build bridges between subject areas. Two examples of how to do this are suggested here.

1. Directions to student: Research information about important dates in the life of a scientist, a mathematician, an author/poet, or an inventor/explorer. Write them up in challenging math problems to be solved by the student. Here is one based on the life of abolitionist, Frederick Douglass.

FREDERICK DOUGLASS

As an author, speaker, and editor, Douglass devoted his life to fighting slavery. See if you can use your math skills to figure out some of the "important dates" in his lifetime.

a. Frederick Douglass was born in the year . . .
   $(6 \times 44) + (11 \times 103) + 421 =$
b. Born a slave in Tuckahoe, Maryland, Douglass was sent to Baltimore to work for a new master whose wife helped him to learn to read and write in . . .
   $(17,283 \text{ divided by } 7) - 643 =$
c. Douglass published his autobiography in . . .
   $(5280 - 1379) - 2056 =$
d. Douglass started an antislavery newspaper called the "North Star" in . . .
   $(62 \times 37) - (333 + 114) =$

2. Directions to student: Research information about facts and figures on a "hot topic" of interest and relevance to students. Use this data as a springboard for creating a variety of word problems for students to solve. Here is an example of this strategy applied in the area of pollution and its subsequent costs to the public.

POLLUTION COSTS

a. The EPA reports that every person in the United States generates approximately 3.5 pounds of garbage in a single day. How much garbage does this individual generate in a week, a month, and a year? How many pounds of garbage is generated by members of your family in one year? In your classroom in one year? In your school in one year?

b. After the Exxon tanker ran aground in the harbor of Valdez, Alaska, the price of gasoline increased almost 15 cents a gallon. If there are 125,000,000 gallons of gasoline used in the United States each day, what was the total cost per day to consumers?

Research information about facts and figures related to a particular unit of study or an important place or event. Again, use these data to construct a set of math challenges for your students that could become part of an interdisciplinary unit. An example of how this could be done is shown on the following page using a science chart and topic about our solar system.

1. How many more million miles is Saturn from the sun than the following planets: Mercury, Venus, Earth, Mars, and Jupiter?
2. What is the total diameter (in miles) of each of the nine planets?
3. How many days is the length of year (in Earth time) for the planets of Jupiter, Saturn, Uranus, and Neptune?
4. How many minutes is the length of day (in Earth time) for Mercury?
5. Convert the temperature of each planet to the Fahrenheit scale.
6. Is the percentage of the weight of an object (100 pounds on Earth) approximately 1 1/2 times greater, 5 times greater, or 10 times greater for Jupiter than for Earth?

Refill as often as necessary

OUR SOLAR SYSTEM

Planet	Distance from Sun (miles)	Moons	Diameter (miles)	Length of Year (in Earth time)	Tempera-ture	Weight of an Object (100 pounds on Earth)
Mercury	36 million	0	3,049	88 days	425○ C	37
Venus	67 million	0	7,565	225 days	450○ C	88
Earth	93 million	1	7,973	365 days	150○ C	100
Mars	142 million	2	4,243	687 days	120○ C	37
Jupiter	484 million	16	89,500	11.9 years	-1300○ C	234
Saturn	887 million	18	75,000	29.5 years	-1800○ C	115
Uranus	1.8 billion	15	32,125	164.1 years	-2150○ C	117
Neptune	2.8 billion	8	30,938	247 years	-2000○ C	118
Pluto	3.7 billion	1	1,875	?	-2500○ C	?

Source: Zeman, A., & Kelly, K. (1994). *Everything you need to know about science homework*. New York: Scholastic Reference. Pp. 86-87.

Math challenge four: Using logic puzzles as a way to integrate math in other subject areas can be very effective with middle level students. Two examples of these are included as reproducible pages following this section. They are entitled:

> 1. Compatibility Chart (Science)
> 2. The Bard Of Britain (Language Arts)

Math challenge five: Combining numbers from a variety of historical events or scientific findings can also be a resource for building bridges between math and another discipline. Below you will find two such examples related to a study of the three branches of government and another related to a study of American history.

1. Start with the number of U.S. Senators; multiply by the number of Supreme Court Justices; add the number of representatives in the House of Representatives; subtract the number of amendments in the Bill of Rights; and divide by the number of years in a U.S. president's term.

2. Start with the year of the founding of Jamestown as a British Colony; add the date (year) of the Boston Tea Party; multiply by the year Andrew Jackson was elected President of the U.S.; and divide by the number of slave states that formed their own government called the Confederacy.

Math challenge six: Flowcharting symbols and methods are often intriguing to middle level students and involve the use of geometric figures in their design. Introduce students to the generic flowchart symbols below and instruct them to use these symbols in constructing a flow chart to show others how to perform a given task such as:

a. How to plan a math party
b. How to solve a word problem
c. How to measure your bedroom for carpeting
d. How to add fractions
e. How to study for a math test
f. How to annoy your math teacher

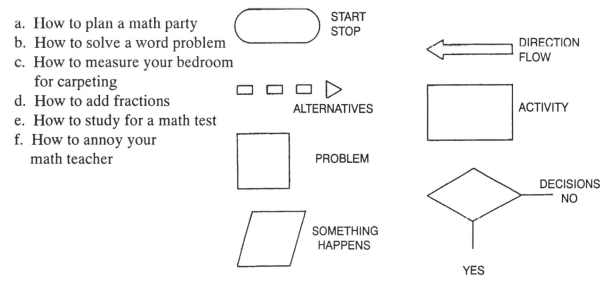

Math challenge seven: Bingo is a popular game with students, but Ann Fisher has created a version of this game that is a little different and that can be adapted to any math topic ranging from whole numbers to decimals. Study the reproducible page entitled "Hey, Bingo Brains!" and use this as a model for designing similar bingo pages for the classroom.

Math challenge eight: Provide students with sets of tangrams that can be made from poster board by enlarging the pattern below. Instruct students to complete a variety of tasks such as the following:

1. Compare and contrast the small triangles with the large triangles. How are they alike and how are they different?
2. Use three small triangles to form a square, a rectangle, a parallelogram, a trapezoid, and a right triangle.
3. Use all or part of the tangram figures to construct as many letters of the alphabet as you can.
4. Determine the cost of the whole tangram puzzle if one of the small triangles costs $20.00.
5. Find the cost of each piece of the tangram if the whole puzzle costs $40.00.

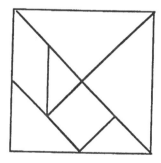

Math challenge nine: Distribute 1 inch square graph paper to each student. The grid should be long enough to provide a row for each child and wide enough to accommodate the longest name in the class, allowing one letter per square. Students should count the number of letters in their first or last names and color in the appropriate number of squares on the graphing grid. They should then complete the grids for the other members of the class accordingly. Students should then be asked to respond to such questions as:

a. Whose name has the fewest or greatest number of letters?
b. How many names have fewer than five letters? more than five letters?
c. Which number of letters do you find more often than any other?
d. How many members of your class have the same number of letters as you do?

 **Math challenge ten:** Use the taxonomies to construct a variety of creative tasks using numbers as the theme. Some sample math activities using Williams' Taxonomy are suggested here:

FLUENCY

a. Using bills and coins, show as many ways as you can to make $10.00.
b. List things that come in twos, threes, and/or fours.

FLEXIBILITY

a. List many different questions that will give you "a dozen" for an answer.
b. Pretend you are the number ten. List many different things you might say.

ORIGINALITY

a. Design a math tee shirt, bumper sticker, or billboard.
b. Create a math superhero and describe his superhuman strengths, skills, and interests.

 **Math challenge eleven:** Have students do comparative shopping projects on favorite apparel items such as sneakers or jeans. They should begin by generating a list of popular brands and then researching the brands in local retail stores to determine price, special features, and quality factors in the merchandise. Students should then use a 10 point scale to rate such categories as style, color, comfort, material, etc. They should then compare the prices with the ratings and make a histogram with two bars — one of the rating, one of the price — for each item.

Refill as often as necessary

Compatibility Chart

Use Your Chart to Answer these Questions:

_____ 1. Mr. O wants to give some blood to some sick patients at the hospital. The following people are in need of a transfusion: Mr. A, Mrs. B, Ms. O, and Sir AB. To whom can he safely give?

_____ 2. Mrs. A wants to give also. These patients are waiting A, B, O, and AB. Which of them can take Mrs. A's blood?

_____ 3. Miss B has just given blood. What blood types should not use her donation?

_____ 4. Mr. AB visited the blood center and donated some blood. Which blood types cannot receive his blood?

_____ 5. Which blood type can give to everyone else, all other blood types, but can only receive his own blood type in return?

_____ 6. A patient with type AB blood needs a transfusion. Which blood types can safely be given to him?

Type O	Receiver A	Receiver B	Receiver O	Receiver AB
Type A	Receiver A	Receiver B	Receiver O	Receiver AB
Type B	Receiver A	Receiver B	Receiver O	Receiver AB
Type AB	Receiver A	Receiver B	Receiver O	Receiver AB

Source: Compatability chart. (1992, Nov./Dec.). *Educational Oasis, 37,* 18. Carthage, IL: Good Apple. (Reproducible Page).

THE BARD OF BRITAIN

Shakespeare wrote his plays for performance, not publication, and apparently took no part in their printing. Shakespeare's lack of interest in each play's publication created problems for historians trying to accurately date each work.

On the basis of historical record, the dates given are the closest estimates that we have of these publications.

Listed below are ten of Shakespeare's more famous plays. Using the clues given, list the plays from the most recently published to the oldest.

1. *MacBeth* is next to *The Tempest*.
2. *Julius Caesar* was published more recently than *Romeo and Juliet*.
3. *Romeo and Juliet* comes between *Julius Caesar* and *The Comedy of Errors*.
4. *The Tempest* is the most recently published play.
5. *Hamlet* is newer than *The Comedy of Errors*, and they were both published after *Richard III* was published.
6. No play comes between *Hamlet* (more recent) and *Twelfth Night*.
7. No play comes between *King Lear* and *Macbeth*.
8. *Twelfth Night* is older than *Othello*, and both are older than *King Lear*.
9. *Othello* is newer than *Hamlet* and both are newer than *Julius Caesar*.
10. *Othello, Hamlet* and *Julius Caesar* are all newer than *The Comedy of Errors*.

Hamlet											1592
The Comedy of Errors											1593
Julius Caesar											1595
King Lear											1599
Romeo and Juliet											1600
Twelfth Night											1601
The Tempest											1604
Richard III											1605
Othello											1606
Macbeth											1612

Source: The bard of Britain. (1988). *Challenge, 32,* 39. Carthage, IL: Good Apple. (Reproducible Page).

Hey, Bingo Brains!

Bingo was "born" over sixty years ago in the month of December. Almost anyone can play Bingo, but can you answer the questions below about this Bingo card?

B	I	N	G	O
14	30	40	57	62
13	21	43	47	65
6	28	FREE	59	61
12	26	44	56	73
10	19	45	60	71

1. Find the row (horizontal) whose numbers yield the highest total. _____

2. Which five numbers have an average of 26? _____

3. Which five numbers are multiples of 4? _____

4. Choose five numbers, one from each column (vertical), that will total 203. _____

5. Choose five numbers, one from each row, whose sum is 181. _____

6. Which five numbers, from anywhere on the board, have a product of 1,146,6000? _____

Source: Fisher, A. (1992). Hey, bingo brains! *Challenge, 48* 35. Carthage, IL: Good Apple. (Reproducible Page).

18. Looking at Common Things in Uncommon Ways

Effective for students who:

• exhibit strength in body–kinesthetic intelligence
• are reading below grade level
• are highly creative and resourceful
• are good problem solvers

Good teachers often see many learning opportunities in unusual situations or with unusual springboards. Sometimes the most common objects can provide material for a lesson plan that will both motivate and challenge students in many ways. The following activities represent common "items" that were used to develop learning tasks for students that require application of basic skills in most subject areas. The possibilities for this strategy are unlimited and the tasks can become part of a learning station, a cooperative learning experience, an interdisciplinary unit, or an individual worksheet.

SPRINGBOARD ONE: Balloons

Directions to student: Use the box of balloons at your table to complete the following tasks and watch your mind "blow up" with many creative ideas.

LANGUAGE ARTS

1. Describe a balloon in detail to someone who has never seen it before. Consider using the five senses as part of this descriptive paragraph.
2. Compose a "parts–of–speech" poem about a balloon. These poems are unrhymed, five–lined, and follow this pattern:
   line 1 – one article (a, an, the) + one noun
   line 2 – one adjective + one conjunction + one adjective
   line 3 – one verb + one conjunction + one verb
   line 4 – one adverb
   line 5 – one noun related to the noun in line 1
3. Locate a list of five fiction books in the media center that deal with balloons as part of the title or as part of a chapter's events. Write these up in an annotated bibliography.
4. Create an autobiography of a balloon at a circus, a birthday party, a political convention, a carnival, a fair, a supermarket opening, or a flea market. Tell all about its adventures and its close encounters with trouble.

5. Read Shel Silverstein's poem "Eight Balloons" in the book *A Light in the Attic.* Draw a picture to go with the poem.

SCIENCE

1. Compare and contrast a helium blimp with a hot air balloon. How are they alike and how are they different?
2. Devise a series of experiments using balloons to demonstrate different scientific principles. Consult your science textbook for ideas. Write your experiments up using the scientific method.
3. Experiment to discover how you can stick a pin in a balloon without popping it.

SOCIAL STUDIES

1. ·Read to find out why Charles Goodyear is associated with the world of balloons. Prepare a comic strip using balloons as the vehicle for reporting facts about him.
2. Create a Rube Goldberg invention to "break a balloon." Include at least five different "chains of events" in your design.
3. Research to discover how balloons are made or manufactured. Show your results in diagram or flow chart format.

EXPLORATORY

1. Experiment to find out how to twist and turn balloons to make balloon critters.
2. Stage a water balloon contest for your class.
3. Create a papier maché object by using a balloon as the form or base.

 SPRINGBOARD TWO: Peanuts

Directions: Use the bowl of peanuts in the center of your table to complete these "nutty" activities.

LANGUAGE ARTS

1. Alliterative sentences contain words that all (or most all) begin with the same letter such as: "Peter picked a peck of pickled peppers." Write an alliterative sentence about peanuts.

2. In a good paragraph, explain how you think each of these "peanut expressions" came into use and what each of them means.
   a. She went "nuts" after she won the award.
   b. He is as "nutty" as a fruitcake.
   c. They are two people who are "nuts" about each other.
   d. That problem is a hard "nut" to crack.

SCIENCE

1. Work with a group of ten other students for this activity and make certain that the bowl at your table holds ten different shelled peanuts — no more and no less. Each student is to randomly select a peanut from the bowl and examine it carefully writing down notes as to the nut's particular attributes. When each student is finished, all nuts are returned to the bowl and mixed together. One by one, each student goes to the bowl and attempts to pick out his/her peanut from the others. Were there any two peanuts exactly alike?
2. Collect five examples of different kinds of nuts from the display table. Compare and contrast each one of these nuts according to their physical characteristics. Put this information in chart form.
3. Research to find out the nutritional value of nuts. Write out your findings on one of the cut out peanut shapes. Use the cookbooks on the display table to locate recipes with nuts as one of the ingredients. Select one to prepare at home or in class. Record the book title, page number, and name of your recipe on your peanut cut out and post on the peanut bulletin board so nobody else will choose your recipe to make. If possible, prepare the recipe at home and bring it in to share with members of the class in a "peanut tasting" party.

SOCIAL STUDIES

1. Use a U.S. map to identify the greatest peanut producing areas in the country. Be able to explain why peanuts are a popular product in those areas. Choose one of these places and create a bumper sticker and/or license plate for that state using a peanut theme.
2. Invent an island in the shape of a peanut. Give it a name and include its major geographical features. Name the cities, rivers, and special places after peanuts. Describe what tourists can do when visiting your island.

MATHEMATICS

1. The average person eats almost 3 pounds of peanuts a year. Determine how many pounds of peanuts are eaten by the people in your class and the people in your school.
2. Visit the supermarket and locate five different bags of five different types of peanuts. Determine which of these is the best "nut" buy and why.

EXPLORATORY

1. Create a peanut puppet or a pet nut (like the pet rock fad of a few years back). Compose a mini–booklet telling others how to care for your peanut puppet or your pet nut.
2. List as many uses for discarded peanut shells as you can think of.

SPRINGBOARD THREE: Combs

Directions: Use the box of combs in the middle of your table to complete each of the following tasks (or use your own comb if it is clean).

LANGUAGE ARTS

1. List as many words as you can think of that end with the letters "mb." Write your words in alphabetical order. Classify your list of words in some way. Write an interesting sentence using as many of your "mb" words as you can and still have it make sense.

2. Answer each of the following "comb" questions giving at least three to five similarities for each one:
   a. How is a comb like a toothbrush?
   b. How is a comb like a stapler?
   c. How is a comb like a skateboard?
   d. How is a comb like a pair of scissors?

3. Compose a conversation that might take place between your comb and the comb of your best friend? your worst enemy?

4. Make a "comb" word–ladder list. You do this by starting with the word "comb" and changing one letter at a time to form a new word. See how many words you can come up with in two minutes. Have someone time you!
   Example: comb, come, cone, cane, etc.

SOCIAL STUDIES

1. Interview a beautician or a barber by telephone or through a personal visit. Make a list of the questions you would want to ask him/her.

2. Research to discover how hair styles have changed over the years. Show your results in picture form.

MATHEMATICS

Count the teeth in your comb. Use this number to complete the following tasks:
   a. How many teeth would there be if you had 7 combs identical to the one you have? if you had three dozen? if you had a gross?
   b. Work with a group of 10 peers and have them all hold their combs up in the air at the same time. Guesstimate the number of teeth in all the combs combined. Check your estimate.

SCIENCE

Read to find information about these other types of "combs" honeycomb, catacomb, coxcomb, and currycomb. Prepare a short report to share your information.

SPRINGBOARD FOUR: Skateboards

Directions: Use the skateboard at your station to complete the following tasks:

LANGUAGE ARTS

1. Write a description of a skateboard without letting your reader know what you are writing about. Write this from the point of view of the skateboard.
2. Do the ABC's of skateboards. Can you think of a word for each letter of the alphabet that relates to the sport of skateboarding?
3. Write a short story using one of the titles suggested here:
   a. *The Skateboard That Got Me In Trouble*
   b. *What I Would Do If My Skateboard Had Magical Powers*
   c. *A Day In The Life Of My Skateboard*
   d. *Everything You Wanted To Know About My Skateboard But Were Afraid To Ask*

SOCIAL STUDIES

1. Give as many reasons as you can think of for the popularity of the skateboard.
2. Define the following words as they are used in the business of selling skateboards. Use complete sentences giving an example of each and using skateboards as the theme: fad, craze, sales, profit, inventory, demand, supply, advertising, and bargain.

SCIENCE

1. Give an example of a scientific principle that you could demonstrate with a skateboard.
2. List the safety precautions that skateboarders should follow when engaging in their sport.
3. Brainstorm things with wheels but no engine, that could be used for travel or to move objects relatively short distances.

MATHEMATICS

1. Design a public skateboarding facility to scale that could be constructed in your community. How big will it be? What shape will it be? What variations in height will there be? What unusual features will it have?
2. Construct a set of math problems related to the world of skateboards. Include an answer key. Two examples are given here:

   —If the average cost of a skateboard is $56.00, what would it cost to buy one for every student in your class? (Don't forget to figure in the sales tax).

   —Estimate how many skateboards there are in your school using the number owned by students in your class as the average.

1. Plan a skateboard contest, exhibition, or school for your class. Make an outline of your ideas and consider such things as:
    a. When and where will it be held?
    b. Who can participate?
    c. What activities will be shared, offered, or demonstrated?
    d. What operating rules will be necessary?
    e. What costs will be generated?
2. Design a fancy "skateboarding" fashion for boys and/or girls. Draw a picture of the finished product.

Refill as often as necessary

19. Discovering the Magic of Language

Effective for students who:

a. are deficient in vocabulary development
b. are interested in "words" and "play on words"
c. exhibit strength in verbal linguistics intelligence

 These activities encourage the creative use of language to build a student's vocabulary and to generate student interest in the magical sounds and multiple meanings of words. Use the starter ideas below as springboards for preparing a variety of language development tasks that could be used as part of creative writing, creative thinking, and creative spelling exercises.

LANGUAGE IDEA ONE: Below are a list of common nouns that you are familiar with. Write a specific example for each noun and be sure to capitalize the words where appropriate to do so.

Sample nouns:

mammal	occupation
amphibian	invention
mineral	timepiece
metal	official
fowl	monument
scientist	desert
chemical	queen

Now, use the list of proper nouns or phrases below and write a corresponding common noun to reflect the proper noun.

Sample nouns:

Shel Silverstein	Spanish
The Call of the Wild	Atlanta Braves
Yankee Doodle	Mona Lisa
"The Road Not Taken"	Picasso
Paul Bunyan	Michael Jackson
Little Miss Muffet	St. Patrick's Day

It should be noted that the words used in this exercise can be from a specific subject area or topic such as the ones above, which are common vocabulary words from the disciplines of science, social studies, language arts, and exploratory courses.

LANGUAGE IDEA TWO: The following groups of words are called "stink pinks" because they consist of rhyming words to fit a given definition. Instruct students to study the examples below and then think of some "stink pinks" of their own.

Examples: naked bunny is a bare hare
bashful insect is a shy fly
chubby feline is a fat cat
musical instrument from Caribbean island is a Cuba tuba
answer to an ecology problem is a pollution solution

LANGUAGE IDEA THREE: The following words represent a set of well–known terms with silly definitions. Share these with students and have them generate "daffynitions" of their own.

Examples: A carpet is any animal who enjoys riding in a car.
A castanet is a way to catch a butterfly.
A pageant is a bug that eats pages in your book.

LANGUAGE IDEA FOUR: It's raining cats and dogs — words, that is. In each set below, the phrase "cat or dog" is part of the spelling of the words or expressions. Check the clues for help.

1.   _ C A T
2.   C A T _ _
3.   C A T _ _ _
4.   C A T _ _ _ _
5.   C A T _ _ _ _ _
6.   C A T _ _ _ _ _ _
7.   C A T _ _ _ _ _ _ _
8.   C A T _ _ _ _ _ _ _ _
9.   _ C A T _ _ _ _ _ _ _ _

Clues: 1. Scram! 2. Got it! 3. Moo! 4. Use it to shop from home 5. In Trivial Pursuit, the orange questions belong in the _____ of Sports 6. A big church 7. A game with string 8. On the diagonal 9. Somebody who can't remember

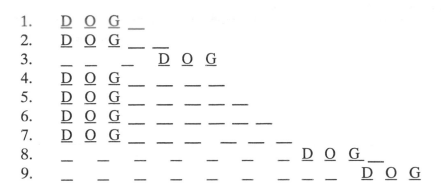

1. D O G __
2. D O G __ __
3. __ __ __ D O G
4. D O G __ __ __ __
5. D O G __ __ __ __ __
6. D O G __ __ __ __ __ __
7. D O G __ __ __ __ __ __ __
8. __ __ __ __ __ __ __ D O G __
9. __ __ __ __ __ __ __ __ __ D O G

Clues: *1. Plural form 2. An orphaned calf 3. Baseball food 4. A way to get around in snowy places 5. Where you end up when you get in trouble 6. A swimming stroke 7. Restaurants give these when people can't finish their meal 8. When nothing goes right 9. A blind person's companion*

ANSWERS:

Cats –

1. Scat 2. Catch 3. Cattle 4. Catalog 5. Category 6. Cathedral
7. Cat's cradle 8. Catty corner 9. Scatterbrain

Dogs –

1. Dogs 2. Dogie 3. Hot dog 4. Dogsled 5. Doghouse 6. Dog paddle
7. Doggie bags 8. Go to the dogs 9. Seeing–eye dog

LANGUAGE IDEA FIVE: Wacky Wordies are familiar words, phrases, sayings or names expressed through a series of rebus drawings. Have students figure out the examples and then come up with ideas of their own.

1. GAME (surrounded by stars)

2. spinal (with cord)

3. (comic with stripes)

4. BAG (A raised above the line)

LANGUAGE IDEA SIX: Using proverbs to stimulate vocabulary development can also be popular with students. One can assign a proverb to a student and have him/her rewrite the proverb using a thesaurus to find synonyms for the words that are more sophisticated and complex. The reverse can be also be used as a vocabulary development exercise.

Examples

Proverb: "Don't put all your eggs in one basket."
Rewrite: "Refrain from depositing your entire supply of poultry products in a single receptacle."

Proverb: "Too many cooks spoil the broth."
Rewrite: "An overabundance of chefs damages the bouillon."

LANGUAGE IDEA SEVEN: Advertising and popular products on the market can also be used to stimulate creative thinking. Instruct students to complete each of the blanks below with the name of a candy bar. Can they supply additional candy bar products using this model? What other products could be used in a similar way?

Example: Fill in the blanks with the name of a candy bar:

a.   _____ is a constellation of stars.

b.   Lewis and _____ led an expedition.

c.   _____ contains two pronouns for girl.

ANSWERS: *Milky Way, Clark, Hershey*

LANGUAGE IDEA EIGHT: Instruct students to think of 26 pairs of opposites whose first letters are the same. Two examples include:
A = ask & answer
B = bare & bountiful

LANGUAGE IDEA NINE: Puns have always been popular with kids and using these in the classroom can be very productive. Have students study the example here and then create some puns of their own.

Examples

a.   All the animals came to the picnic in pairs except the worms. They came in apples.
b.   "I don't understand why this coffee tastes like mud," said Mr. Walker. "It was ground only this morning."

c.   It was not surprising that the octopus won the battle, since he went into it well–armed.

d.   The sailor did not have to worry about his dirty clothes. He just threw them overboard and they were washed ashore.

LANGUAGE IDEA TEN: "Tom Swifty" jokes humorously combine a quotation and the verb or verb and adverb describing the way it was said. Share these examples of the "Tom Swifty" concept and have them create some of their own.

Examples:

a.   "You say you've struck oil?" she gushed.

b.   "Drop that gun," the man said disarmingly.

c.   "Watch out for the spear," he said pointedly.

d.   "I'll turn you into a frog," she said charmingly.

Refill as often as necessary

20. Holiday Happenings

Effective for students who:

- respond well to "teachable moments"
- enjoy "mini–disciplinary" units
- exhibit strength in the interpersonal intelligence

 Calendars are filled with well–known and not–so–well–known holidays. These dates can be used successfully to structure a variety of learning tasks that require students to apply basic skills within the context or guise of a holiday event. Samples of the types of activities a teacher might want to model are included here for a few common holidays. These holidays make excellent themes for a one day interdisciplinary unit.

EXAMPLE ONE: *Thanksgiving*

a. Write an editorial from a turkey's point of view explaining why its life should be spared.

b. Using your five senses, describe a Thanksgiving feast.

c. Research to find out what the following individuals had to do with the Pilgrims landing on Plymouth Rock and the evolution of Thanksgiving as a holiday:

> William Bradford
> Squanto
> Samoset
> Ben Franklin
> Explorer Thomas Dermer
> Sarah Josepha Hale
> Massasoit

d. Generate a list of 50 ways for a turkey to escape being served for Thanksgiving dinner.

e. The First Thanksgiving was celebrated in 1621. How many years ago was this celebration? How many decades? How many years must pass before your answer is equal to five centuries?

f. What if the Pilgrims had not had turkey on Thanksgiving Day, but hot dogs? How would our traditions be different?

g.   What if the wild turkey, not the eagle, was our national symbol?

h.   Write a short newspaper from a turkey's point of view called *The Gobbler Gazette.* Be sure to include a news story, feature story, editorial, want ad, display ad, comic strip, and horoscope.

i.   Design a postage stamp or first day cover to commemorate the Thanksgiving holiday.

EXAMPLE TWO: Halloween

a.   Create a blueprint of a haunted house according to scale. What shape will it be? How many rooms will it have? What will the rooms look like? What activities will be featured in each room?

b.   Compile a catalog for a ghost much like the catalogs from Sears or Penny's. What is the name of your catalog company and where is it located? What items will you carry and how will you describe them for the prospective buyer, the witch? How much will they cost and how are they to be used?

c.   Plan a Thanksgiving menu for a witch including gourmet food items that would appeal to this character. Make sure that all four food groups are represented.

d.   Stage a contest to guesstimate how many pumpkin seeds or candy corn pieces are in a given receptacle.

e.   Design a travel brochure for a family of black "bats and cats" who want you to visit their spooky barn on Halloween night.

f.   Make a list of Halloween costumes that would appeal to boys and girls your age who have been invited to a Halloween party. Survey your classmates to determine which ideas are most appealing to them. Graph your results.

g.   Collect Halloween poems and short stories. Schedule a time when students in your class turn out the lights, get comfortable, and take turns reading the selections to one another using scary voices and expressions.

h.   Rewrite the "Twelve Days of Christmas" so that the words and lyrics reflect the "Twelve Days of Halloween."

i.   The American Broom Manufacturing Company has gone on strike. Brainstorm at least ten other things that a witch could use on Halloween instead of a broom.

j.   Design a greeting card to a vampire. Use Halloween words, puns, messages, and symbols in your creation.

k.   Create a booklet of "beauty tips" for a witch to use to make herself ugly on Halloween.

EXAMPLE THREE: *St. Patrick's Day*

a. Plan a menu of all green foods for St. Patrick's Day. Try to represent all four food groups for a nutritious meal.

b. Write a creative story about the "day it rained shamrocks."

c. Design a collage of "green things." Give your artistic collage a special title and write a descriptive paragraph about it with green crayon, colored pencil, or magic marker.

d. Research to find out all you can about Ireland. Design a travel folder to share your information.

e. Design a "Wanted Poster" for a lost leprechaun.

f. Construct a trivia game around St. Patrick's Day. Two questions to get you started are:
   . . . What is a shillelagh?
   . . . What are the three colors in Ireland's flag?

g. Many people associate a "three leaf clover" with good luck. Compose a legend to explain this superstition.

EXAMPLE FOUR: *Easter*

a. Think up 25 uses for an empty egg carton.

b. Create an Easter bonnet or cap that would appeal to students your age.

c. Make up a list of "egg" words that are modifications of real words such as: eggsiting, eggocentric, and eggazeration.

d. If you could fill the most wonderful Easter basket for yourself, what would you want to receive in it?

e. Create a WEB of ideas around the holiday, Easter.

f. Plan an Easter Egg hunt for a group of children.

g. Discover ways you might color and decorate eggs if you had no dye.

h. Think of ways you might stage a practical and successful Easter egg toss.

i. Design an experiment to test this idea: Do or can eggs float?
   Hint: Things can float in liquids besides water.

Refill as often as necessary

21. Response or Learning Journals

Effective for students who:

- exhibit strength in the intrapersonal intelligence
- need practice in writing
- have difficulty expressing their attitudes, opinions, or ideas
- are visual learners

 A response journal or learning log is basically a written dialogue in which students record their personal reactions to, questions about, reflections on, and experiences with varied learning tasks. It is important that students receive feedback from the teacher on their journal entries which can be done in the same amount of time teachers take for correcting papers or preparing lesson plans. Teachers can introduce journal writing in a variety of ways and use them for a variety of assignments. Common types of responses that could be required are outlined below, although the options are unlimited.

Responding to the Textbook

1. Your reaction to a paragraph, section, or chapter
2. Your summary of information from a paragraph, section, or chapter
3. Your opinion of the material written or chapter format
4. Your feelings about the illustrations, tables, and figures
5. What you wish the textbook would have included that it did not
6. What you felt as you learned the information
7. What you liked and disliked about the material
8. Questions you have after reading the material

Responding to a Literary Assignment

1. Opinions about the setting, plot, or characters
2. Expressions of emotions such as enjoyment or boredom
3. Comments on the language or literary techniques used
4. Comparisons of the text with the reader's own life
5. Predictions as to what will happen next
6. Reflections on the reading process

7. Questions about vocabulary, plot, or character's behavior
8. What surprised you about the section you read today?
9. With what characters do you identify with most?
10. What unusual words, phrases, expressions, or images did you find that you liked or that you would like clarified?

Responding to a Self–Assessment

1. When I come to a word I don't know I . . .
2. What I do best as a reader is . . .
3. What I would like to do better as a reader is . . .
4. What I do when I read something important is . . .
5. What I have trouble understanding in this chapter or section is . .

Responding to Quotations

1. "Babies of all nations are alike until adults teach them." (Mauree Applegate)
   RESPONSE TASK: What does this statement mean to you? What prejudices or stereotypes do you observe in other people around you or in yourself? Where do you think these came from? What can we or you do about them?

2. "Change is one form of hope; to risk change is to believe in tomorrow." (Linda Ellerbee)
   RESPONSE TASK: Do you welcome change or do you avoid it? Give examples to support your answer. What excites you about the future and what scares you about the future?
3. "I cannot pretend to feel impartial about colors. I rejoice with the brilliant ones and am genuinely sorry for the poor browns. (Winston Churchill)
   RESPONSE TASK: What colors do you rejoice in and what colors do you feel sorry for? What color do you have on today; why did you choose it? How does it make you feel?
4. "Television is chewing gum for the eyes." (Frank Lloyd Wright)
   RESPONSE TASK: Do you agree or disagree with Frank Lloyd Wright's opinion of television? In what ways is television chewing gum for the eyes?

Responding to Creative Prompts in Subject Areas

1. Explain ways in which the weather has some direct effect on your life?
2. If you were a blue whale and could talk, what would you say to human beings?
3. Imagine you had a chance to talk to a gladiator during Roman times. List the questions you would ask him.

4. When you see a picture of the White House, what thoughts go through your mind?
5. What do you think you could learn from an ant?
6. List the ways that you could help to reduce racial bias and discrimination in your school?
7. Do you think recycling is important or just a waste of time?
8. Explain why you do or do not believe in UFO's?
9. What invention do you wish you had discovered and why?

10. If you could live in another country for a year, where would you want to go? Give reasons for your answer.
11. Which of the following explorers have made the greatest impact on our world?
12. What would you like to know about the people who live in New Zealand?
13. Write whatever comes to your mind when you read the following Chinese proverb: "With time and patience, the mulberry leaf becomes a silk gown."
14. What advice would you give to someone running for public office in your community?
15. Write everything you know about acids and bases.
16. Who is a hero of yours? Explain why that person means so much to you.
17. List the three most important facts you learned today about the American Revolution.
18. Which would you rather be: a circle or a square? Why?
19. Write about a social issue that you feel strongly about. Explain why you feel this way.
20. Based on what you now know about computers, make five predictions about what it will be able to do in the future.
21. Explain how you go about solving a word problem in math.
22. Describe the work you did on the electricity experiment.
23. Summarize what is most important to understand about the area and perimeter of shapes.
24. Something I would really like to know about outer space would be . . .
25. Tell how you know your solution to the problem is right.
26. What is the relationship of this to that?
27. What were the scientific ideas in this experiment?
28. The following lines are from the poem "The Walrus and the Carpenter" by Lewis Carroll: ''The time has come,' the Walrus said, 'To talk of many things: Of shoes — and ships — and sealing wax — Of cabbages and kings —' List all of the things you would like to talk about.
29. In John F. Kennedy's address, he said, "And so, my fellow Americans: Ask not what your country can do for you — ask what you can do for your country." What would you most want to do for your country if you could?
30. If you lived in another country, why might you want to immigrate to the United States?

Refill as often as necessary

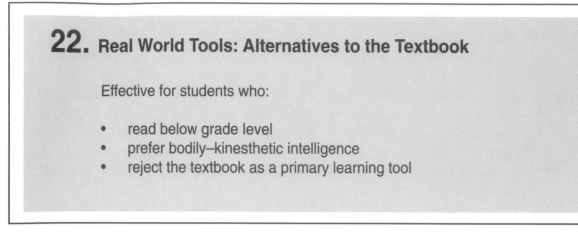

22. Real World Tools: Alternatives to the Textbook

Effective for students who:

- read below grade level
- prefer bodily–kinesthetic intelligence
- reject the textbook as a primary learning tool

 Using real world tools and resources as "substitute textbooks" for teaching or reinforcing basic skills can be very effective with many students. They can also be used as part of learning stations, cooperative learning group tasks, and individual study projects. Although one can use an unlimited number of these springboards in the classroom, only four are included here as examples to illustrate the process. Other resource materials to consider using in this context are: Catalogs, Directories, Travel Folders, Magazines, Recipe Books, or How–To Manuals.

REAL WORLD TOOL ONE: **Menus**

Directions: Use the collection of menus assigned to your table for completing each of these activities. Keep your work in a folder labeled " You Are What You Eat."

KNOWLEDGE TASKS:
1. Record the names of the restaurants represented in your group's collection of menus.
2. List the varied types of information which are included on the menus.
3. State things the restaurant owners have done to make their menus attractive and/or interesting.

COMPREHENSION TASKS:
1. Describe the multiple purposes of a menu.
2. Explain why some restaurants use their menus as part of a newspaper ad or post it in a showcase outside their establishment.
3. Summarize the process for how you and members of your family select a restaurant when you eat out for a meal.

APPLICATION TASKS

1. Select one of the menus and use it to do the following:
   a. Determine what items you would select from the menu to make up five different and desirable meals for you that would total no more than $46.35 and no less than 43.00 (give or take a few cents).
   b. Decide what entree is most appealing to you and how many quarters you would need to pay for it.
   c. Develop a meal for yourself that would require payment of 20 quarters, 20 dimes, and 20 nickels.

2. Select a menu with lots of desserts. Pretend you have won a free dessert for a week. There are only two catches: You can't have the same thing more than once and you can't have a dessert with an even number of syllables. List your seven choices, price of each, and the number of syllables in a simple chart. Then add the prices together to get a total cost for the week and find the average cost per day. Finally, if you had been allowed to order the same dessert for each of the seven days, which dessert would you have chosen and what would the total bill cost?

   Note: If the restaurant has limited dessert choices, then add some of your own to complete this activity.

3. To do this activity, prepare a sheet of paper with each letter of the alphabet written on the lines in a vertical column along the right hand side of the page. Locate an interesting or appealing dish from any of the menus for each of the letters and write its cost on the appropriate line. When you have "finished eating your way" through the alphabet, figure out the total cost of the foods which spell:

   your first or last name
   vowels only
   every other letter
   the words "I'm stuffed"

ANALYSIS TASKS:

1. Pretend it's your birthday and you have invited 10 friends to go out to eat with you. Two friends are your age; two friends are much younger than you; two friends are not more than 10 years older than you; and two are over 65. Decide which restaurant in the menu collection would be best for this group and speculate as to what each person is most likely to order according to his/her personality, tastes, or age.

2. Analyze each of the menus in your collection and determine what are the "best buys" or "best values" in foods for each restaurant.

3. Analyze each of the menus in your collection and determine the "worst sounding meals" from each menu. Determine how much you will save by not ordering them.

SYNTHESIS TASKS:

1. Pretend you are going to open up a special restaurant for "kids" your age. What will you name it and where will it be located? What unique theme or decor will it have? What unusual meals/mouth watering descriptions will if offer? What creative services will it provide? Design a menu that has a different shape, print style, and format to fit your restaurant theme.

2. Compose a short commercial, magazine ad, or billboard for one of the restaurants in your collection.

3. Design a series of "learning place mats" that could be used in any of the restaurants of your collection. What topic will you choose and what facts will you share about that topic?

EVALUATION TASKS:

1. Rank order the restaurants in your menu collection from your least favorite to your most favorite. Give reasons for your choices.

2. Decide on whether you would rate the restaurants in your menu collection as a one star, two star, three star, or four star restaurant. Establish criteria for each level before assigning the rating.

3. Defend or negate this proverb: "Too many cooks spoil the broth."

REAL WORLD TOOL TWO: **Cereal Boxes**

FLUENCY: List as many different types of information or offers as you can find on the boxes of cereal in your collection.

FLEXIBILITY: Classify these information types and offers in some way and explain your classification scheme.

ORIGINALITY: Tell about the most unusual item you found on one of the cereal boxes that did not appear on any of the others.

ELABORATION: Expand on this statement about cereals using data from your cereal box collection: Cereals are one of the most nutritious foods you can eat and one of the most economical treats you can buy.

RISK TAKING: If you had to be one of these types of cereals in a box, which one would you want to be and why: A fruit loop, a cocoa krispie, an oat square, a corn flake, a shredded wheat, or a cheerio.

COMPLEXITY: It has been said that Americans have too many choices when shopping for food at the supermarket which is especially true of products like cereal. Explain why Americans have so much and other Third World countries have so little.

CURIOSITY: What if all cereals manufactured had to be packaged in exactly the same way so that they all looked alike except for the name. What do you think would happen to cereal sales and production?

IMAGINATION: Visualize yourself as the creator of a brand new cereal for The Quaker Oats Company in Chicago, Illinois. Describe what it would look like, taste like, sound like, feel like, and smell like. Design a box for it and make the package as informative and as interesting as you can.

BONUS TASK: Pretend you are a math teacher and you have the challenge of creating a math lesson using the information on one of the cereal boxes. Select a box of cereal from the collection, assume the role of your math teacher, and develop a set of math computation and word problems around the information presented. Be sure to include an answer key!

REAL WORLD TOOL THREE: **Yellow Pages**

Directions: Use the collection of cereal boxes assigned to your group as the information source for completing these tasks.

READING: Survey the Yellow Pages and explain what varied types of information are found in these pages as well as how the information is organized and presented. Decide what features of the Yellow Pages make it easy to read or hard to read from a customer's perspective. Then, practice your reading skills and locate an entry that appeals to you for each of the following situations. Write down your responses in chart form recording the name of the business, the address, a reason for your choice, and the number of the page where you found it.
- You want to take your dog to be clipped and groomed.
- You want to locate entertainment for your guests at your next birthday party.
- You lost the key to your house and need help.
- You have broken your leg and need crutches.
- You would like to buy an inner tube to take on your beach vacation.
- You want to surprise your mother with flowers for Mother's Day.
- You want to have your minibike repaired.
- You want to plan a field trip to an interesting place in your community.
- You want to locate a restaurant that you have never heard of and that serves Mexican food.
- You want to locate a place to buy model airplanes to make.

SOCIAL STUDIES: It has been said that the Yellow Pages are a marketplace for consumers. Define marketplace and explain why this is likely to be true.

SCIENCE: Locate a variety of resources that could be used in the teaching of a life science topic, a physical science topic, and an earth science topic. Select one of these topics and outline a plan for using resources from the Yellow Pages to deliver this lesson.

MATHEMATICS: Find out what it costs to advertise in the Yellow Pages. Determine the total advertising costs for any two pages in the Yellow Pages.

ART: Create an unusual Yellow Page ad for a business of your choice. What can you do to make it appealing to someone using the Yellow Pages to locate a resource?

REAL WORLD TOOL FOUR: **Newspapers**

Directions: You will be studying the local newspaper during this mini–unit, and each day your group will receive five copies of the newspaper to be used for completing this two week assignment. Please note that each of you will be asked to maintain a scrapbook of newspaper clippings for the week and, as a culminating activity, your group will be creating a King Size Front Page of a classroom newspaper that encompasses your best thinking and application of newspaper reporting/writing skills. Use the pieces of manilla drawing paper in the center of your table as the inside pages of your scrapbook and the colored pages as your cover. You may staple your pages together upon completion of the scrapbook tasks. Each group will be given a long piece of white shelf paper for their King Size Front Page.

SCRAPBOOK TASK ONE: Use the reference books at the Newspaper Center to create a glossary of newspaper terms. The following concepts are to be included in your glossary complete with definitions. Record these on the first page of your scrapbook.

Banner	Display ad	Letters to the Editor
By–line	Editorial	News story
Caption	Feature story	Obituary
Classified ad	Headline	Syndicated column
Copy	Index	Weather report
	Lead	

FRONT PAGE TASK ONE: Your group will be creating a King–Size Front Page newspaper around a theme or topic of your choice. The "extra long" piece of shelf paper is to be used for this purpose and rolled up scroll style when it is completed. Use fine line magic markers for writing up all newspaper copy. The first task for your group is to think of a theme and then choose a name for your newspaper that relates to the theme. For example, if you want to do a newspaper around the Revolutionary War, then your newspaper might be *The Revolutionary Times*. If you want to do a newspaper around outer space, then your newspaper might be *The Space Gazette*. If you want to do a newspaper with a literary theme, then your newspaper might be *The Book News*. If you want to do a newspaper around the world of computers, then your newspaper might be *The Technology Tribune*.

SCRAPBOOK TASK TWO: Use the newspaper to locate the banner headline and news story of the day. Cut and paste it in your scrapbook on page two. Next to the story, write the 5 W's of the information given answering these questions:

Who is it about?	What happened?
When did it take place?	Why did it happen?
Where did it take place?	How did it happen?

FRONT PAGE TASK TWO: Write a news story about an event related to the theme of your newspaper, making certain to include the five W's and How. Each member of your group should write his/her own news story.

SCRAPBOOK TASK THREE: Use the newspaper to locate a feature story in one of the sections. Cut and paste it in your scrapbook on page three. Next to the story, write the 5 W's of the information given answering these questions:

Who is it about?	Why did it happen?
Where did it take place?	When did it happen?
What happened?	How did it happen?

FRONT PAGE TASK THREE: Write a feature or human interest story related to the theme of your newspaper, making certain to include the five W's and How. Each member of your group should write his/her own feature story.

SCRAPBOOK TASK FOUR: Use the newspaper to locate an Editorial and a Letter to the Editor. Cut and paste these items in your scrapbook on page four. Next to the Editorial, write a reaction to the ideas presented by the editor in a good paragraph stating your position or opinion on the subject under discussion. Then, write a Letter to the Editor responding to the one pasted in your scrapbook.

FRONT PAGE TASK FOUR: Write an Editorial and a Letter to the Editor on a subject related to the theme of your newspaper, making certain to support your opinions or feelings with documented facts and statistics. Again, each member of your group should write his/her own editorial and letter to the editor.

SCRAPBOOK TASK FIVE: Use the newspaper to locate a display advertisement and a set of at least five classified ads of special interest to you. Cut these out and paste them on page five of your scrapbook. Next to the display ad, analyze the strengths and weaknesses of the ads as a prospective consumer of the product or service. Make suggestions for improving the ad if possible. Next to each classified ad, write a sentence or two telling whether you would be interested in responding to the ad and why or why not.

FRONT PAGE TASK FIVE: Create both a display ad and a classified ad related to the theme of your newspaper. Make certain each member of your group designs his/her own pair of ads.

SCRAPBOOK TASK SIX: Use the newspaper to locate the obituary column and paste it on page six of your scrapbook. Analyze the ads and figure the average age of the people who died on that given day. Show your computation next to the article.

FRONT PAGE TASK SIX: Write an obituary for a fictitious "someone" that could have died from a natural cause or accident related to the theme of your newspaper. Make certain each member writes his/her own fictitious obituary for this assignment.

SCRAPBOOK SEVEN: Use the newspaper and locate a syndicated column such as an advice column, a health column, a financial column, or a sports column. Cut out and paste it on page seven of your scrapbook. Imitate the columnist's style, and try to write a similar column of your own next to the original one.

FRONT PAGE TASK SEVEN: Pretend you are a famous columnist and write a syndicated column in an area of your own choosing but related to the theme of your newspaper. Each member of your group is to write his/her own column.

SCRAPBOOK EIGHT: Use the newspaper and locate the weather report for the day. Cut and paste it on page eight of your scrapbook. Write a paragraph summarizing the weather for today in your area and in ten other cities around the country. Try to write your comments rebus style including pictures for words where appropriate to do so.

FRONT PAGE TASK EIGHT: Write a weather report that is appropriate for the theme of your newspaper. The group should write the report together including various graphs and charts that typically appear in the weather report section.

SCRAPBOOK NINE: Use the newspaper and locate a photograph of special interest to you. Cut and paste it in your scrapbook. Write a short "lead" about the photograph using the caption as a hint or source of information.

FRONT PAGE TASK NINE: Draw a picture to serve as a photograph around the theme of your newspaper. Include a caption. Each member of your group should contribute a "picture photo" of their own.

SCRAPBOOK TEN: Use the newspaper and locate three or four comic strips that you enjoy reading. Cut and paste them in your scrapbook. Write a sentence or two next to each one, stating why you think this comic strip is a good one and what techniques each writer uses to get his ideas and humor across.

FRONT PAGE TASK TEN: Create a comic strip of your own related to the theme of the newspaper. Each group member should create his/her own comic character.

SCRAPBOOK ELEVEN: Use the newspaper and locate a sports story of special interest to you. Analyze all of the sports stories in this section and make a list of words, phrases, and sentences that include words, terms, or expressions that are unique to sports writing.

FRONT PAGE TASK ELEVEN: Write a sports story that is appropriate to your newspaper theme. Each group member should create his/her own comic character.

SCRAPBOOK TWELVE: Use the newspaper and locate a book review, a play/ movie review, a restaurant review, or a review of some other type. Cut and paste it in your scrapbook. Write a statement summarizing the position of the reviewer.

FRONT PAGE TASK TWELVE: Select a fiction or nonfiction picture book from the media center related to the theme of your newspaper. Read it and write a review of it for your newspaper. Each group member should write his/her own review.

Refill as often as necessary

Teachers can design a wide variety of thematic projects around student interests and aptitudes by employing a "unit in a box" concept. Specifically, the teacher determines the topics for these box projects, collects the information sources to be used in the box projects, and designs one or more task cards outlining the nature of the activities to be completed in the box projects.

Two box project units are included here as reproducible pages. The first thematic project is entitled "Colorful Geography" and the Box Contents are: (1) U.S. Map; (2) Information Sheets: "Color Me Thinking About Geography" and "Where in the United States Is"; and (3) Task Cards for Weeks One Through Six.

The second thematic project is entitled "Colorful Art" and, again, uses the topic of "color" as the organizing theme for integrating subject areas. The Box Contents for this project are: (1) A set of postcards of famous paintings (available from any book store) or a set of prints (available from any poster company); (2) Art supplies such as magic markers, colored pencils, crayons, colored chalk, and water colors; and (3) Task Card.

Refill as often as necessary

Color Me Thinking About Geography —

...Brownville, Clay, Coffee, Evergreen, Graysville, Greene, Green Pond, Greensboro, Greenville, Red Bay, and Red Level, **ALABAMA?**

...Copper Center and Sand Point, **ALASKA?**

...Ash, Black Canyon City, Greenlee, Green Valley, and Peach Springs, **ARIZONA?**

...Almond, Black Rock, Calico Rock, Cherry Valley, Clay, Greenbrier, Greene, Green Forest, Greenland, Greenwood, Pumpkin, Strawberry, and White, **ARKANSAS?**

...Blue Lake, Cherry Valley, Greenbrae, Greenfield, Greenville, Orange, Orange Cove, Orangevale, Pumpkin Center, Red Bluff, Redding, Red Hill, Redlands, Redway, Redway City, and Walnut, **CALIFORNIA.**

...Black Forest, Black Hawk, Evergreen, Golden, Redcliff, Red Feather Lakes, and Silverton, **COLORADO?**

...Blue Hills, Ivoryton, Orange, and Redding, **CONNECTICUT?**

...Green Acres, **DELAWARE?**

...Cape Coral, Cocoa, Cocoa Beach, Coral Cove, Coral Gables, Coral Springs, Coral Way Village, Golden Beach, Golden Gate, Greenacres City, Green Cove Springs, and Greensfort, **FLORIDA?**

...Peachtree City and White, **GEORGIA?**

...Pearl City, **HAWAII?**

...Blackfoot and Silverton, **IDAHO?**

...Blue Island, Blue Mound, Brownstown, Green Oaks, Green Rock, Greenup, Green Valley, Greenview, Greenville, Red Bud, White Hall, White Pines, and Whiteside, **ILLINOIS?**

...Black Oak, Brownsburg, Greencastle, Greendale, Greenfield, Greensburg, Greentown, Redkey, Rosedale, Roseland, and Silver Lake, **INDIANA?**

...Blue Grass, Greenfield, Greenfield Plaza, Redfield, and Walnut, **IOWA?**

...Blue Rapids, Greenleaf, Greenburg, Rosehill, Silver Lake, Walnut, White City, and Whitewater, **KANSAS?**

...Ashland, Auburn, Cherrywood Village, Gray, Graymoor, Grays Knob, Grayson, Greensburg, Greenup, Greenville, Hazel, Silver Grove, White Plains, Whitesburg, and Whitesville, **KENTUCKY?**

...Golden Meadow, Gray, Grayson, Greensburg, Pearl River, Red Oak, Red River, Rosedale, Roseland, Rosepine, Vermillion, and White Castle, **LOUISIANA?**

...Auburn, Ashland, Blue Hill, Brownville, Brownville Junction, Gray, Greenville, and Limestone, **MAINE?**

...Coral Hills, Greenbelt, Green Haven, Greensboro, Sandy, Silver Hill, Silver Springs, White Marsh, White Oak, and White Plains, **MARYLAND?**

...Auburn, Cherry Valley, Greenfield, Green Harbor, Orange, Silver Lake, and White Island, **MASSACHUSETTS?**

...Auburn, Auburn Hills, Grayling, Greenville, Hazel Park, Olivet, Pearl Beach, Redford, Roseville, White Cloud, Whitehall, White Pigeon, and White Pine, **MICHIGAN?**

...Blackduck, Blue Earth, Brownsdale, Browns Valley, Brownton, Golden Valley, Greenbush, Redlake, Red Lake Falls, Red Wing, Redwood Falls, Rosemount, Roseville, Silver Bay, Silver Lake, Walnut Grove, White Bear, and White Bear Lake, **MINNESOTA?**

...Blue Mountain, Coffeeville, Golden, Greenville, Greenwood, Hazlehurst, Mt. Olive, Olive Branch, Orange Grove, Pearl, Pearlington, Red Banks, Rosedale, Silver City, Walnut, and Walnut Grove, **MISSISSIPPI?**

...Black Jack, Blue Springs, Blue Summit, Bowling Green, Golden City, Green City, Greendale, Greenfield, Greenwood, Hazelwood, and Olivette, **MISSOURI?**

...Black Eagle, Browning, Evergreen, Golden Valley, Red Lodge, Rosebud, West Yellowstone, Whitefish, White Sulphur, and Yellowstone, **MONTANA?**

...Auburn, Blue Hill, Blue Springs, Brown, Cherry, Clay, Greenwood, Red Cloud, Redington, Sterling, Silver Creek, and Whiteclay, **NEBRASKA?**

...Ash Meadows Rancho, Ash Springs, Blue Jay, Cherry Creek, Coaldale, Crystal Bay, Gold Point, Goldfield, Emeralde, Ruby Valley, Silver City, Silver Peak, Silver Springs, and White Pine, **NEVADA?**

...Greenfield, Greenland, Greenville, and Whitefield, **NEW HAMPSHIRE?**

Source: Johnson, N.L. (1992). *Thinking is the key: Questioning makes the difference.* Beaver Creek, OH: Pieces of Learning. Creative Learning Consultants, pp. 35-39. ($10.95, $3.50 s/h. Pieces of Learning, 1610 Brook Lynn Drive, Beavercreek, OH 45432-1906)

Where in the United States is...

...Browns Mills, Browntown, Cherry Hill, Cinnaminson, East Orange, Greenfields, Little Silver, Maple Shade, Maplewood, Orange, Red Bank, Roseland, South Orange, West Orange, White Horse, and White Meadow, **NEW JERSEY**?

Black Lake, Black Rock, Bluewater, Crystal, Golden, Greenfield, Greenville, Melrose, Red Hill, Red River, Silver City, White Horse, White Lakes, White Rock, and Whites City, **NEW MEXICO**?

...Black River, Blue Point, Brownsville, East Greenbush, Greene, Green Island, Greenlawn, Greenport, Greenville, Greenwich, Greenwood Lake, Lake Carmel, Maplewood, Orange, Orangeburg, Orange Lake, Pearl River, Pine Bush, Pine City, Pine Island, Pine Plains, Red Hook, Red Oaks Mill, Rosendale, Silver Center, Silver Springs, White Plains, Whitesboro, and White Sulphur Springs, **NEW YORK**?

...Ash, Asheboro, Asheville, Ashland, Black Mountain, Cherryville, Goldsboro, Granite Falls, Greensboro, Greenville, Hazelwood, Mount Olive, Pine Grove, Pinebluff, Pinetops, Pineville, Piney Wood, Red Springs, Rose Hill, Roseboro, Silver City, Southern Pines, Tarboro, Toast, Walnut Cove, White Lake, and Whiteville, **NORTH CAROLINA**?

...Ashley, Hazleton, Lemmon, and Roseglen, **NORTH DAKOTA**?

...Amberley, Amberly, Black Horse, Blacklick Estates, Bowling Green, Brown Heights, Cherry Grove, Crystal Lakes, Greenfield, Greenhills, Green Springs, Greentown, Greenview, Greenville, Greenwich, Maple Heights, Marble Cliff, Marblehead, Mt. Carmel, Mt. Carmel Heights, Mt. Sterling, Orange, Redbud, Rosemount, Roseville, Rubyville, Silver Lake, Silverton,

Whitehall, Whitehouse, White Oak, and Yellow Springs, **OHIO**?

...Blackwell, Blue, Cotton, Granite, Gray, Greenfield, Red Oak, Rose, South Coffeyville, and Whitefield, **OKLAHOMA**?

...Ashland, Blue River, Brownsboro, Brownsville, Gold Beach, Green, La Pine, Pine Creek, Quartz Mountain, Redmond, Roseburg, and Silverton, **OREGON**?

...Ashland, Black Lick, Brownsville, Cherry Hill, Coaldale, Cranberry, East Greenville, Greencastle, Greensburg, Greenville, Hazelton, Montrose, Mount Carmel, Mount Chestnut, Oliver, Pine Grove, Port Carbon, Red Hill, Red Lion, Sandy, Sterling Run, White Haven, Whitesburg, and Yellow Spring, **PENNSYLVANIA**?

...Ashaway, Ashton, East Greenwich, and Mapleville, **RHODE ISLAND**?

...Blacksburg, Blackville, Bowling Green, Brownsville, Gray Court, Green Sea, Greenville, Greenwood, Orangeburg, and White Oak, **SOUTH CAROLINA**?

...Cottonwood, Pine Ridge, Red Elm, Redfield, Redig, Vermillion, White Lake, White Owl, White River, and Whitewood, **SOUTH DAKOTA**?

...Ashland City, Ashwood, Gray, Graysville, Greeneville, Greenfield, Green Hill, Mt. Carmel, Mt. Olive, Red Bank, Red Bolling Springs, Strawberry Plains, White Bluff, White House, White Pine, Whiteside, and Whiteville, **TENNESSEE**?

...Blue Mound, Brown, Brownfield, Brownsboro, Brownsville, Brownwood, Crystal City, Grapeland, Grapevine, Grayson, Greenville, Honey Grove, Maple,

Marble Falls, Orange, Orange Grove, Pine Springs, Pineland, Piney Point, Red Hill, Redland, Redwater, Rosebud, Rosenburg, Sand Ridge, Sanderson, Santa Rosa, Red Water, Rose City, Silver, Silverton, Sterling City, White Deer, Whitehouse, White Oak, Whitesboro, White Settlement, and Whitewright, **TEXAS**?

...Black Rock, Green River, Greenwich, Mt. Carmel, Mt. Carmel Junction, Orangeville, Redmond, Rosette, Silver City, Snowville, Sterling, and Whiterocks, **UTAH**?

...Orange and White River Junction, **VERMONT**?

...Ashland, Blacksburg, Blackstone, Bluefield, Blue Ridge, Bowling Green, Greenville, Orange, Rose Hill, Rustburg, Sterling, and White Stone, **VIRGINIA**?

...Auburn, Black Diamond, Browns Point, Granite Falls, Grayland, Grays Harbor, Greenacres, Navy Yard City, Rosalia, Ruston, Silverdale, Salmon Center, White Center, and White Samon, **WASHINGTON**?

...Bluefield, Clay, Whitesville, and White Sulphur, **WEST VIRGINIA**?

...Ashland, Black Center, Black Earth, Black River Falls, Brown Deer, Green Bay, Greendale, Greenfield, Green Lake, Greenwood, Hazel Green, Redgranite, Spring Green, Whitefish Bay, and Whitewater, **WISCONSIN**?

...Graybull and Greenriver, **WYOMING**?

Source: Johnson, N.L. (1992). *Thinking is the key: Questioning makes the difference.* Beaver Creek, OH: Pieces of Learning. Creative Learning Consultants, pp. 35-39. ($10.95, $3.50 s/h. Pieces of Learning, 1610 Brook Lynn Drive, Beavercreek, OH 45432-1906)

Color Town

Color Me . . . Asking Questions!

Week One

How far is it from Strawberry Plains, Tennessee to Strawberry, Arkansas?
In your opinion, which town/city has the most colorful name in the United States?

Would you rather live in White Owl, South Dakota or White Deer, Texas? Why?

Design a logo for Brown Deer, Wisconsin or Grapevine, Texas.

Which color is the most popular in the list of towns? How does it feel to be popular? Is there an unpopular color town? Make a list of questions an unpopular color town might ask a popular color town.

Find East Orange, Orange, and South Orange, New Jersey. Why isn't there a West Orange or North Orange, New Jersey?

What would you do if you wanted to delay or lose a letter in the United States mail? What if you forgot to write the name of the state and zip code on the envelope? Which town name would you use that would guarantee confusion in the post office?

Week Two

Pretend you are feeling very sad. Which color town would you visit? Why?

Which town is larger—Pumpkin Center, California or Pumpkin, Arkansas?

Think about the colors black, gray and white. If Gray, Oklahoma is the "between color" town, what might the towns on either side be? Name the "between color" town that is between Brownsborro, Oregon and Orange, Connecticut. (Amberly, Ohio) Name the "between color" town that is between Coffee, Alabama and Redmond, Utah. (Auburn, Nebraska)

Pretend you are visiting Pearl City, Hawaii. List all the contents of your suitcase.

White House, Tennessee is angry at Whitehouse, Texas. What's the problem?

Compare/contrast Blacklick Estates, Ohio, with Black Lick, Pennsylvania.

What if Copper Center, Alaska and Cocoa Beach, Florida could be sister cities? Write a letter from one to the other.

Research the history of Graybull, Wyoming. Design a postage stamp in its honor.

Source: Johnson, N.L. (1992). *Thinking is the key: Questioning makes the difference.* Beaver Creek, OH: Pieces of Learning. Creative Learning Consultants, pp. 35-39. ($10.95, $3.50 s/h. Pieces of Learning, 1610 Brook Lynn Drive, Beavercreek, OH 45432-1906)

Week Three

What if you were a fish? Which color town would you like to live in? Why?

Which state has the greatest percentage of color towns? Which has the smallest? Count all the color towns in all the states. Graph your results.

Combine your favorite color with your name and create a new town name. Construct a collage that represents your personal color town.

Write several color town names on small pieces of paper. Put them in a sack. Shake them up. Take turns with a friend drawing from the sack. How fast can you or your friend find the color town on a map?

Categorize the color towns into color families by creating mindMaps. Use the primary colors of red, yellow and blue as the focus for each mindMap. Can you think of other ways to categorize or mind-Map the color towns?

List the color towns that make you feel like laughing; those that make you scared; and those that make you question or feel puzzled.

In your opinion which color town names are the most ordinary? Which are the most unusual? Make two lists. Compare/contrast your list with a friend's list.

Week Four

Create a large color wheel. Use paint or construction paper. Write several color town names on the color wheel. Where should Vermillion, South Dakota be written on your wheel?

Compose a list of What would happen if...? questions about the color towns.

Using a box of crayons, rename each crayon by using the list of color towns. Is there a Mount Chestnut, Pennsylvania in your box? List things that should be colored with Mount Chestnut.

What if Red Feather Lakes, Colorado got stuck in Tarboro, North Carolina?

Reds, oranges, and yellows are warm colors. Choose a color town that is warm and draw a picture of it using only reds, oranges, and yellows. Blues, purples, and greens are cool colors. Choose a color town that is cool and draw a picture of it using only blues, purples, and greens.

Congratulations! You have just won a free trip to White River Junction, Vermont. From your home, list the states you will travel through on the most direct route and on the longer, more scenic route. Fill out a time schedule for each day of your vacation. What did you do on Tuesday at 3:00 pm?

Source: Johnson, N.L. (1992). *Thinking is the key: Questioning makes the difference.* Beaver Creek, OH: Pieces of Learning. Creative Learning Consultants, pp. 35-39. ($10.95, $3.50 s/h. Pieces of Learning, 1610 Brook Lynn Drive, Beavercreek, OH 45432-1906)

Week Five

Write a story about Hazel Green who lives in Hazel Green, Wisconsin.

List all the color towns that taste good or smell good.

Design a new tourist attraction for Coffeeville, Mississippi. Create a travel brochure that will entice visitors to your attraction.

Compose a list of quantity questions about the color towns. Your questions might begin with the following: How many ways could....? What are all the ways....? How many different....?

Is there a real white castle in White Castle, Louisiana? How could you find out? Can you buy a White Castle hamburger in White Castle?

Survey your family and neighborhood. List all the towns/cities each person has ever lived in. Any color towns?

Oh no! Navy Yard City, Washington has just been quarantined. Why?

Week Six

Create a new professional sports league. Each team is based in a color town. List the towns and names of each team.

Write a story or poem that has five color towns mentioned in it.

Follow, follow, follow the yellow brick road to: (list all the yellow color towns)

Create colorful names for all the streets and avenues in Greenup, Kentucky.

Design a color town quilt. Ask your friends to design a block for your quilt.

Using the melody from the country song, "I've Been Everywhere" by Hank Snow or Lynn Anderson, compose a color town song.

Compose a color town "rap." Choreograph a dance to go with it.

Source: Johnson, N.L. (1992). *Thinking is the key: Questioning makes the difference.* Beaver Creek, OH: Pieces of Learning. Creative Learning Consultants, pp. 35-39. ($10.95, $3.50 s/h. Pieces of Learning, 1610 Brook Lynn Drive, Beavercreek, OH 45432-1906)

TASK CARD FOR "COLORFUL ART"

1. Examine the art materials in your box. Practice drawing something with each one of them. Describe the advantages and disadvantages of using each art material.

2. Classify or group the paintings in your box in some way. Explain your classification scheme.

3. Compare and contrast any two paintings on the same subject or by the same artist. In how many ways are they different? In how many ways are they the same?

4. Write a poem or story about one of the paintings. What do you think is happening?

5. Describe where you would go to see the original of some of the paintings in your collection. Locate the cities on a map.

6. Select a painting and try to draw one like it using one of the art materials in your box.

7. Select a historical period and study this period through its art. Determine all of the things you can learn about the period by analyzing its painting, sculpture, and architecture.

8. Organize a school art gallery for your classmates. Where will the gallery be housed? Compute the area needed to showcase the art work. What criteria will you use for judging which art will be accepted for display?

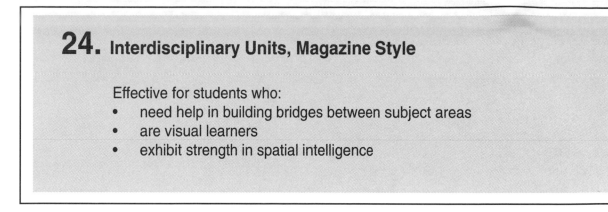

24. Interdisciplinary Units, Magazine Style

Effective for students who:
- need help in building bridges between subject areas
- are visual learners
- exhibit strength in spatial intelligence

 Integrating subject areas through mini–units that can be done in a day or a week are often effective ways to help students see the relationships that exist in the various disciplines. These mini–units can be done in small cooperative learning groups, as enrichment learning centers, for homework assignments, or as independent study tasks. Using a magazine format in designing the mini–unit tasks can be visually stimulating to the student and can serve as a disguise for the amount of student effort required to complete the tasks.

Two such interdisciplinary units are provided here as reproducible pages — one on "Flight" and one on "Numbers."

Refill as often as necessary

FLIGHT

1. List as many different things as you can think of that fly. Classify the items on your list in some way.

_____

_____

_____

_____

_____

_____

2. Compare a flying hero of mythology with a modern comic strip hero of today.

_____

_____

_____

_____

_____

3. Create a new design for the outside of a hot air balloon.

5. Design a paper airplane contest for your class. Where will it be held? Who can enter? What categories will you include? Design an invitation to enter the contest and a certificate for winning one of the contest entry sessions.

_____

_____

_____

_____

_____

_____

_____

_____

_____

_____

_____

_____

_____

_____

_____

4. Create a time line illustrating the important dates in the history of flight.

_____

6. Write down all of the jobs that are involved with a single airline flight from the booking of the flight to arriving at a destination. Rank order the jobs from the most important to the least important.

_____

_____

_____

_____

_____

10. Pretend you were a reporter covering an historic moment in aviation such as the Kitty Hawk with the Wright brothers, Lindberg's landing in France, or Armstrong's splashdown from space. Describe the event.

7. What would happen if all airports were shut down because of air pollution and/or air space crowding of the skies. Predict all consequences for society. Develop strategies for dealing with the situation.

_____

_____

_____

_____

_____

_____

_____

_____

_____

_____

_____

_____

8. Write down five terms associated with the concept of "flight" and define each one.

_____

_____

_____

_____

9. Record the words of a popular song or poem associated with a flight theme.

_____

_____

_____

_____

NUMBERS

1. Write a number autobiography about yourself. Consider all the different numbers that are important to you such as address, weight, birth date, favorite radio station, bike registration number, etc.

_____

_____

_____

2. Create a secret code using mathematical symbols and/or operations. Write a message in your secret code.

_____

_____

1...2...3...4

3. Compile a list of statistical facts on a topic of your choice where numbers "tell a story."

_____

_____

_____

4. Plan a political campaign to have your favorite number selected as the "national number" for the United States.

_____

_____

_____

_____

_____

_____

_____

5. Explain what you think these "number-related" statements mean:

a. His number is up.

_____

_____

_____

b. Her days are numbered.

_____

_____

c. The numbers don't support it.

_____

_____

d. I've got her number!

_____

_____

6.   Design a set of original number patterns for others to complete.

7.   Create a wallpaper or fabric design using only numbers or numerals.

8.   List as many careers as you can think of that require a comprehensive mathematical background because they deal with numbers.

_____

_____

_____

_____

_____

ΠιΙη ΘΛ

9.   Write an original story to explain why "13" is considered to be an unlucky number while "7" is considered to be a very lucky number.

_____

_____

_____

_____

_____

_____

_____

_____

10.   It's your turn to write a math problem. Using four operations one time each (one addition, one subtraction, one multiplication, and one division operation), write a math problem that results in your zip code, your telephone number, or today's date.

_____

_____

_____

_____

_____

_____

_____

25. Starter Sentence Sparklers

Effective for students who:

- have difficulty expressing their personal beliefs or feelings
- exhibit strength in intrapersonal intelligence
- respond well to starter ideas for expressing themselves in writing

Using sentence stems or starters can be an excellent tool for motivating students to write about their personal feelings or for directing students to respond to a catalyst for writing ideas. These starter sentences are most effective when they are designed around a particular theme or topic such as conflict, anger, decisions, or problem solving. They can also be effective when used to introduce or review a unit of study. Several examples of sentence stems that "spark" the minds and imaginations of students are suggested below.

Starter Sentences For Decision Making
- Whenever I am forced to make a decision I feel . . .
- Making decisions is hard for me because . . .
- I enjoy making decisions about . . .
- The best decision I ever made was . . .
- A decision I made that "backfired" was . . .
- I hope I never have to make a decision about . . .
- I hate it when I make a decision and . . .
- I like it when I make a decision and . . .

Starter Sentences For Anger
- When I am angry, I usually express myself by . . .
- A better way to express my anger would be to . . .
- I feel angry when my teachers (parents, friends) . . .
- When I'm angry at my teachers, I often . . .
- When someone is angry at me, I tend to . . .
- After expressing my anger, I feel . . .
- Some things that really make me angry are . . .

- The angriest I have ever been was when . . .
- A time when I controlled my anger was . . .
- Anger can be destructive because . . .

Starter Sentences For Problem Solving
- Solving problems is easy (or hard) for me because . . .
- The skills I need most to solve problems are . . .
- The ability to solve problems is important when . . .
- A time I solved a problem effectively was . . .
- A time when I tried to solve a problem too soon was . . .
- A time when I faced a serious problem on my own was . . .

Starter Sentences For Introducing A Unit On Weather
- Something that interests me most about studying the weather would be
- An important weather fact I already know is . . .
- I will read about or listen to a weather report when . . .
- The weather is very important to some people because . . .
- The best reason I can think of for studying the weather would be . . .

Starter Sentences For Reviewing A Unit On Weather
- Five facts I learned about weather from this unit were . .
- The most interesting thing we did in class during our weather unit was
- The hardest thing for me to learn or remember about the weather had to be . . .
- Something we learned about the weather but that I would like to know more about is . . .
- One thing I am going to do as a result of our weather unit is . . .

Refill as often as necessary

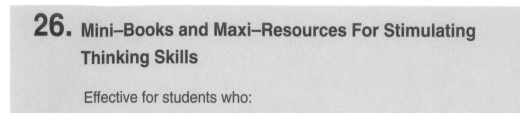

26. Mini–Books and Maxi–Resources For Stimulating Thinking Skills

Effective for students who:

- enjoy knowing or learning about trivia
- exhibit strength in logical/mathematical intelligence
- respond to unusual stimuli as instructional tools

 Teachers can use a wide variety of mini–books and paperback resources found in most major book stores as unusual tools for stimulating creative thought in the classroom. These reading references are designed to "tease the minds" and "stretch the imaginations" of their readers and, therefore, are perfect springboards for getting middle level students to make inferences, predictions, and judgments.

MINI–SPRINGBOARD ONE: Parker, T. (1987). *Rules of thumb.* Boston: Houghton Mifflin Company.

SYNOPSIS: This book is a collection of "rules of thumb" which the author describes as "homemade recipes for making a guess. They are easy–to–remember guides that fall somewhere between a mathematical formula and a shot in the dark." Use one or more of these "rules of thumb" as springboards for: (1) Testing the rule to see if it works; (2) Inferring how it came to be; and/or (3) Analyzing the logic behind it.

a. "Rule of Thumb" 1: WRITING A POEM: When you're writing a poem, eliminate nine out of ten adjectives and adverbs in the first draft, and cut everything you've heard before.

b. "Rule of Thumb" 2: WATERING YOUR PLANTS: For watering houseplants, when in doubt, don't. But for plants on your patio or windowsill, when in doubt, do.

c. "Rule of Thumb" 3: POPPING CORN: Before making popcorn, check the temperature of the oil by putting three kernels in the pot as it heats; when all three pop, the oil is hot enough. Also, you should get thirty–four cups of popcorn from a cup of kernels. Top–quality kernels will give you an extra ten cups.

d. "Rule of Thumb" 4: EXPLAINING A MATH THEOREM: If you can't explain a mathematical theorem to a ten–year–old, you don't understand it yourself.

e. "Rule of Thumb" 5: FALLING ASLEEP TO MUSIC: If you want to fall asleep with the stereo on, turn the volume down to a level that is too quiet for when you are awake. In less than five minutes, that level will feel comfortable, but if you're still awake in fifteen minutes, you may have to turn the volume down again.

MINI–SPRINGBOARD TWO: Feldman, D. (1988). *Why do clocks run clockwise? And other imponderables.* New York: Harper & Row.

SYNOPSIS: In this book, you will find the answers to questions that you have always wondered about and never had time to find out. The author has compiled information about a wide variety of topics that range from the interesting to the ridiculous. Use this book to locate interesting questions and then speculate on the answers before "reading" the real solution to these imponderables.

Imponderable 1: *WHY do ants tend to congregate on sidewalks?*
(1) Some species, particularly one actually called "pavement ants," prefer to nest on sidewalks and under rocks and other hard surfaces. (2) As John J. Suarez, technical manager of the National Pest Control Association, so elegantly put it: "Sidewalks are a favorite place for people to drop candy, fast food, food wrappers and soft drink containers." Ants are known for their industriousness, but they aren't dumb. If they are given offerings that require no effort on their part, they won't decline the largess. (3) Ants release pheromones, a perfume trail left from the nest to food sources. Pheromones are easily detected on sidewalks, which, as we have already learned, are often repositories for food. Ants on sidewalks, then, are often merely picking up the scent left by scouts before them. (4) Sidewalks absorb and store heat. Ants run around naked. They prefer warmth. (5) The most popular explanation: darkish ants are more easily visible in contrast to the white sidewalk than on grass or dirt. Suarez speculates that the greater warmth of sidewalks may make the ants more active as well as more visible. But don't assume that because you can't see ants on your front lawn they aren't there. THEY ARE EVERYWHERE.

Imponderable 2: *WHY do bananas, unlike other fruits, grow upward?*
If you knew about the tumultuous birth process of the banana, perhaps you would be more charitable the next time you encounter some bruised specimens at the supermarket. The banana is actually a giant herb in the same biological family as lilies, orchids, and palms. It is the largest plant on earth without a woody stem — a banana stalk is 93 percent water — and is consequently extremely fragile. Although it can reach a full height of fifteen to thirty feet in one year, even moderate winds can blow down a plant. The fruit stem or bunch originates at ground level. At this stage, the bunch consists of all of the fruit enclosed in leaf bracts. The individual fruit "fingers" (the technical name for a single banana) are pointed upward. As the bunch or bud is pushing its way through the mass of tightly packed leaf sheaths known as the pseudostem, the fruit fingers remain pointed upward until they emerge at the top of the plant. The bananas exert tremendous

pressure on the pseudostem. Before the fruits expand, the leaves enclosing them roll around on themselves inside the trunk. After the fruit emerges from the leaves, the fingers point downward, but only because the bud surrounding them has changed direction. Once the entire bunch of bananas is mature, fully emerged from its sheath, and pointing downward, the individual leaf bracts enclosing the hands (the female flower cluster) fall away, exposing the fruit. At this point, the individual flowers grow rapidly, filling out. Their increased weight bends the main stalk so that the individual fruits on the hand start to turn upward in about seven to ten days. Dr. Pedro Sole, of Chickadee Bananas, points out that in the past, "primitive bananas grew upwards, like the seeds of most grasses forming a spike." So is there a logical reason for the banana's tortuous up–and–down birthing process now? Jack D. DeMent, of the Dole Fresh Fruit Company, sees the answer in the behavior of the traditional noncommercial banana plant: "A flower is found on the tip of each individual fruit. This flower is removed during [commercial] packing but is present during fruit development. As the hand turns up, the flower is better exposed to insects and nectar eating birds and bats. Their feeding would normally aid in fertilization of the fruit. Today's commercial banana is sterile and rarely – almost never – produces a viable seed." DeMent theorizes that the commercial banana's tendency to grow upward is a holdover from its ancestors that needed to point upward for their very survival.

Presumably, natural selection will simplify the growth process of the banana over the next few hundred thousand years or so.

Imponderable 3: *HOW and WHY do horses sleep standing up?*

Horses have a unique system of interlocking ligaments and bones in their legs, which serves as a sling to suspend their body weight without strain while their muscles are completely relaxed. Thus, horses don't have to exert any energy consciously to remain standing — their legs are locked in the proper position during sleep. Most horses do most of their sleeping while standing, but patterns differ. Veterinarians we spoke to said it was not unusual for horses to stand continuously for as long as a month, or more. Because horses are heavy but have relatively fragile bones, lying in one position for a long time can cause muscle cramps. While one can only speculate about why the horse's body evolved in this fashion, most experts believe that wild horses slept while standing for defensive purposes. Wayne O. Kester, D. V. M., executive director of the American Association of Equine Practitioners, told us that in the wild, the horse's chief means of protection and escape from predators was its speed. "They were much less vulnerable while standing and much less apt to be caught by surprise than when lying down."

Imponderable 4: *WHY are there more brown M&M's than any other color, and how do they determine the ratio of colors?*

M&M/Mars conducts market research to answer precisely these types of questions. Consumers have shown a consistent preference for brown M&M's, so they predominate.

Imponderable 5: *WHY are rain clouds dark?*

Rain is water. Water is light in color. Rain clouds are full of water. Therefore, rain clouds should be light. Impeccable logic, but wrong. Obviously, there are always water particles in clouds. But when the particles of water are small, they reflect light and are perceived as white. When water particles become large enough to form raindrops, however, they absorb light and appear dark to us below.

MINI SPRINGBOARD THREE: Stock, G. (1988). *The kids' book of questions.* New York: Workman Publishing.

SYNOPSIS: This book poses a wide variety of "hard" questions for students to answer on topics ranging from what's right and what's wrong to dilemmas about why parents act as they do. These questions are fun to answer because they challenge students to let people know what they think and they raise issues that kids like to discuss. Use this book to present students with a "question of the day" that will encourage them to share their views and their feelings with one another. Five sample questions from the book are outlined below.

QUESTION ONE: Do you think boys or girls have it easier and why?
QUESTION TWO: Some adults have a lot of trouble enjoying themselves. If you were asked to give them some advice about how to play and have more fun, what would you say?
QUESTION THREE: What is the biggest difference between what happens on television and what happens in the real world?
QUESTION FOUR: What is the hardest thing about growing up?
QUESTION FIVE: If, by wishing it, you could have every person in the world wake up and have the same color skin, would you want that to happen? Explain.

MINI SPRINGBOARD FOUR: Weiss, D. E. (1988). *100% American.* New York: Poseidon Press.

SYNOPSIS: The American people — their character, institutions, habits, beliefs, and opinions — have been captured in this collection of over 1500 surprising, sometimes alarming, often hilarious facts about how we live, love, eat, think, dress, play, shop, sleep, vote, worry, diet, dream and die — all told in percentages of Americans from 1% to 100%. Use this book to share some of these outrageous or humbling facts with the students and have them speculate to both the "causes" and the "effects" of such statistics. What do they say about American values, ethics, character, or life styles?

FACT ONE: 22% of Americans aged 8 to 17 think their parents expect too much of them.
FACT TWO: 46% of Americans think people who have lived in America illegally for several years should be deported.

FACT THREE: 64% of Americans strongly believe that government regulation is needed to protect people from dangerous products.

FACT FOUR: 82% of American teenagers say that homework makes them anxious.

FACT FIVE: 94% of Americans with children in the home hope the children go on to do things they never did.

MINI SPRINGBOARD FIVE: Burnam, T. (1988). *The dictionary of misinformation.* New York, Harper & Row.

SYNOPSIS: This book contains hundreds of entries from A to Z that presents information to refute common myths and perceptions that people have about every conceivable subject from errors in advertisements to documenting evidence that the bagpipe was not a Scottish invention. Use this book with the students to locate pieces of "misinformation" that are related to a topic being studied as part of an instructional unit. Students may even want to write their own version of "The Dictionary of Misinformation" about things they have encountered in their own lives and studies. Two sample pieces of "misinformation" from the book are cited below.

a. MISINFORMATION PIECE ONE: Blacks in the American Colonies.
Not all blacks in colonial American were impoverished slaves. Some were not only both free and wealthy; they even owned slaves of their own, imported by them from their own homeland, Africa. Some imported servants from England until 1670, when the Virginia Assembly made it illegal for blacks to own white servants. Those blacks who were free, or slaveholders themselves, had been emancipated by their owners: some as a reward for faithful service, others as a result of religious convictions somewhat tardily come to by their white owners.

b. MISINFORMATION PIECE TWO: Truth about Lie Detectors.
The devices commonly called "lie detectors" do not, and cannot, actually identify lies. All they can do is to record certain physiological phenomena associated with lying — abnormal respiration, heartbeat, perspiration, for example. It is a crucial, not a frivolous, distinction to recognize that a lie detector's evidence, no matter how skilled the operator, is always inferential, never direct. That is why its findings are taken with a grain of salt by lawyers and judges. And it can be fooled. Persons who are truly unaware that they are lying, when in fact they are, cannot be caught by such a device.

Refill as often as necessary

27. Lists That Teach

Effective for students who:

- prefer lists to paragraphs for learning and recording information
- have short attention spans
- are reading below grade level
- are creative thinkers

 "Lists" can be used successfully in the classroom as instructional tools for teaching a diversity of reading and writing skills in any content area. Four strategies are shown below which can be adapted to a variety of topics within a given discipline by selecting terms, concepts, events, and/or skills most appropriate for that topic.

LIST EXAMPLE ONE: Randomly select an item in Column A and another in Column B. Describe at least five ways these two items are alike.

Column A	Column B
Bat	Teacher
Pair of Socks	Quilt
Student	Wooden Fence
Chair	Floor
Finger	Hammer
Roller Blades	Sweater
Whale	Paint Brush
Marketplace	Pelican
Guitar	Sandpaper

LIST EXAMPLE TWO: Use your textbook and write down ten facts from the chapter you have been assigned. Write down ten opinions you have based on the facts from the chapter. Mix up these facts and opinions and record them in Column A. Work with a partner and ask him/her to decide whether each sentence is a Fact or Opinion in Column B. Have your partner give reasons for his/her response in Column C.

Column A	Column B	Column C
Statement	Fact or Opinion	Reasons

LIST EXAMPLE THREE: In writing a paragraph about a topic, think of many interesting words related to that topic. Make an ABC list of these words and then "plug" these into the sentences wherever appropriate to do so.

A	J	S
B Blanket	K	T Thunderstorms
C	L	U
D Drizzle	M	V
E	N	W
F	O	X
G	P	Y
H	Q	Z
I	R	

BEGINNING PARAGRAPH ABOUT CLOUDS

A cloud can be a stratus cloud which is a low blanket of cloud that often brings drizzle. A cloud that is a cumulonimbus cloud is likely to bring thunderstorms with rain, snow or hail.

LIST EXAMPLE FOUR: Inventions most often occur when someone needs to combine an OBJECT with a PROCESS in a new ENVIRONMENT. Select random numbers to fill in the blanks of the sentence below. Use the first digit for the number to fill in the blank numbered "1," the second digit to fill in the blank numbered "2," and the third digit to fill in the blank numbered "3." Then, read the sentence and do what it says!

Column A Process	*Column B* Object	*Column C* Environment
What does it do?	***What does it do it to?***	***Where does it happen?***
1. transport	1. a hippopotamus	1. on the moon
2. wash	2. a jackhammer	2. in outer space
3. paint	3. a computer	3. in a jungle
4. chill	4. a motorcycle	4. in an art mu seum
5. throw	5. a bouquet of flowers	5. at the top of a skyscraper
6. hide	6. a beehive	6. in your room at home
7. measure	7. a washing machine	7. in a library
8. dry off	8. a cookie	8. in a fire station
9. pulverize	9. a fried egg	9. in a desert

Invent a machine that will:

_____   _____   _____
         a.   b.   c.

Draw a picture of your invention and write a few sentences explaining how it works.

_____

_____

_____

_____

_____

_____

_____

_____

Adapted from: Barden, C. (1993). *Powerthink*. Grand Junction, CO: American Teaching Aids, Good Neighbor Press, Inc.

LIST EXAMPLE FIVE: Combine one word in Column A with another word from Column B, Column C, and Column D to write a sentence showing the relationship between these four words or concepts. The words may be used in any order and you can insert additional words to create a meaningful statement. You are to write five different sentences using one word from each column but not using any word more than once.

calorie	scale(s)	temperature	centigrade
fahrenheit	heat	32 degrees	212 degrees
freezing pt.	boiling pt.	absolute zero	thermostat
measurement	water	scientists	convert

Sample Sentence: Words To Use: *fahrenheit*, *scale*, *temperature*, and *centigrade*. A fahrenheit and a centigrade scale are often used to measure body temperature.

Refill as often as necessary

28. Take Home Learning Kits

Effective for students who:

- are kinesthetic learners
- would benefit from home learning activities
- enjoy "learning by doing" and interactive tasks

The purpose of Home Learning Kits is to provide students and their families with a series of interactive and motivating units to do collaboratively at home and to investigate topics of mutual interest across the disciplines. These kits should be built around themes that are appropriate for the grade level and that are related to topics being studied as part of the regular curriculum. It is suggested that teachers select no more than four different kit topics at one time — one in math, social studies, language arts, and science — and construct multiple copies of each kit topic. Parents can be introduced to the Home Learning Kit concept through a parent letter sent to the home, through a parent mini–inservice session at school, or through a kit fair for parents and their children at school. It is important to solicit parent support of the program so as to acquaint parents with their role in the learning process as well as their responsibilities for the care of the kit materials. Some major decisions that the teacher will have to make when developing this program are such things as:

What kit topics are best to begin the program?
How many kits will be constructed for each topic?
How often are the kits available for check out and check in?
What supplies and materials are needed for each kit?
How will the kits be packaged and maintained?
What kind of parent involvement and orientation is required?
Who coordinates and supervises the kit program?

It is best to house the kits in plastic file boxes that are inexpensive, durable, attractive, and portable. It is important that all materials, equipment, and instructions for completing the kit activities be stored in the kits. Common household items are not included in the kits because they should be readily available.

The contents of the kits should be:
a. **A Parent Suggestion Card** that includes tips on the use and care of the kits.
b. **A Background Information Card** that gives the objectives of the kit, an overview of the concepts to be learned in doing the kit activities, a list of the materials included/needed, and a set of vocabulary words related to the kit's content.
c. **A Reproducible Student Booklet** that contains the directions and worksheets for completing the kit's hands—on activities.
d. **A Simple Evaluation Form** for the family to assess the kit's activities and impact.

SAMPLE PARENT SUGGESTION CARD

GUIDELINES FOR USING KIT
1. Please plan to spend 30 to 60 minutes nightly with your teenager on this kit.
2. Take time to discuss and listen to each other's ideas and suggestions for completing the kit activities together.
3. Ask one another questions such as:
   What is happening?
   Why do you feel as you do?
   How could we approach this differently?
   Where have we experienced this before?
   Can you predict what will happen next?
   What do you think would happen if we . . .?
   Why do people . . . ?
4. Have fun and enjoy the challenge!

REMINDERS WHEN USING KIT
1. Most of the activities and discussion questions are designed to be open—ended with no right or wrong answers.
2. These activities and discussion questions were developed to go along with our study topics in class.

SAMPLE BACKGROUND INFORMATION CARD

OBJECTIVES

1. After completing this kit, the student will be able to draw conclusions about the television viewing habits of the family.
2. After completing this kit, the student will be able to identify and analyze the varied types of television shows which are offered for viewing on prime time.
3. After completing this kit, the student will be able to explain the consequences of too much "teeveeitis" in a family.
4. After completing this kit, the student will be able to experiment with alternative activities to be substituted successfully for television viewing.

OVERVIEW

Television is one of the most exciting inventions of our lifetime because it informs, entertains, keeps people up–to–date, makes them think, tickles their imaginations, and brings beauty to them in many forms. On the other hand, television has also been destructive in many ways especially when it comes to family life and living. Turning on the television set has become an automatic reflex that controls much of what a family does for entertainment and relaxation, eliminating other meaningful activities such as reading, talking, playing, and interacting. Families need to take charge of their television viewing and evaluate WHY they watch it, HOW MUCH they watch it, and WHAT they watch. In short, it is important that individuals gain control of the television set and learn to use it wisely and positively. This kit is designed to help you do just that!

MATERIALS IN KIT
Television Guide from Weekly Newspaper
TV Guide
Graph Paper
Box of Colored Pencils
Hand Pencil Sharpener

SAMPLE KIT ACTIVITIES

Activity 1: *Social Studies: Self–Awareness*

Procedure:

1.   Maintain a weekly log of your family's television viewing habits. For each day of the week, record the names of all television shows that family members watch, the channel on which each show is found, the time that each program is shown, and a brief reaction to the theme of each show.

2.   Organize this information into a chart and draw some conclusions about the viewing habits of your family by completing the starter statement: "From my TV viewing log we learned that . . ."

Activity 2: *Math: TV Guide Search*

Procedure:

1.   Browse through your local TV guide and write down the name of a popular show for each of the following program categories:

Dramas	News Programs	Serials or Soap Operas
Cartoons	Sports Programs	Comedy Series Programs
Talk Shows	Crime or Detective	Adventure Shows
Game Shows	Documentaries	Science Fiction
Educational		or Fantasy
Programs		

2.   Choose a day during the week to calculate the number of shows for each program category and record your results in a large pie or circle graph.

Activity 3: *Language Arts: Writing A Review*

Choose a favorite situation comedy, drama, adventure, crime, or science fiction show to watch. Write a simple review of the show, describing each of the following program elements:

Characters: List the major characters in the show. Tell how they look, act, speak, and feel about one another.

Setting: Describe the basic setting of the show. Discuss the time of year and day the action is taking place as well as how the setting helps create the mood or feeling of the story.

Conflict: Summarize the problem, argument, or disagreement that is causing a conflict between the major characters. Tell how the conflict is resolved.

Plot: Explain three major events in the order that they happened in the story.

Theme: Write a sentence that states the primary message or purpose of the story.

Logic: Determine what parts of the story could really happen and what parts of the story seem unlikely to happen in real–life situations.

Activity 4: *Social Studies: Stereotypes on TV*

Television often promotes false impressions of specific people and their roles or personalities. These are called stereotypes. Think about all the television programs, especially situation comedies and crime shows, that you watch. If you were a visitor from outer space and the only information you had about Americans was what you observed from watching television, what false impressions might you develop about life in the U S? Write your ideas in a short essay.

Activity 5: *Science: Camera Views and Angles*

Television cameras can make the characters and events that they photograph appear in interesting ways. Draw a picture of a tree and show it from the following camera angles:

1.   A long–shot view that shows the full length of the tree and much of its surroundings.
2.   A close–up view that shows only a part of the tree and very little of its surroundings.
3.   A tilted–up view that shows the tree from the ground up.
4.   A tilted–down view that shows the tree from very high up.

Optional Activity 6: *News Shows*

View several daily news shows and make a list of the most common news personalities. Decide what characteristics you feel are important for a news anchor to have and write these down. Create a rating scale from 1 to 10. Develop a line graph figure similar to the one shown that compares the news personalities with one another. Put the characteristics to be rated along the horizontal axis and the rating scale along the vertical axis. Provide a color scale assigning a different color to each person and connect the points on the scale to give you a summary of your results.

Characteristics to be rated

10					
9					
8					
7					
6					
5					
4					
3					
2					
1					
0					

Source: Forte, I., & Schurr, S. (1994). *Interdisciplinary units and projects for thematic instruction.* Nashville, TN: Incentive Publications, Inc., pp. 17, 18-21

Refill as often as necessary

BIBLIOGRAPHY

Barden, C. (1993). *Powerthink.* Grand Junction, CO: American Teaching Aids, Good Neighbor Press, Inc.

Bourman, A. (1989). *61 cooperative learning activities: Thinking, writing, and speaking skills.* Portland, ME: J. Weston Walch, Publisher.

Burgess, M. S. (1988, Sept./Oct.). Learning styles: Using the three e's to develop self–esteem in early teens. *Team 3*(1), 16.

Burnam, T. (1988). *The dictionary of misinformation.* New York: Harper & Row.

Coleman, V. (1988). *Know yourself: 940 questions that uncover the real you!* New York: Fawcett Crest.

Feldman, D. (1988). *Why do clocks run clockwise? and other imponderables.* New York: Harper & Row.

Fischer, M. W. (1993). *World history simulations.* Huntington Beach, CA: Teacher Created Materials.

Forte, I., & Schurr, S. (1993). *The definitive middle school.* Nashville, TN: Incentive Publications, Inc..

Forte, I., & Schurr, S. (1994). *Interdisciplinary units and projects for thematic instruction.* Nashville, TN: Incentive Publications, Inc.

Forte, I., & Schurr, S. (1987). *Science mind stretchers.* Nashville, TN: Incentive Publications, Inc.

Gall, M. D. (1973, February). What effects do teachers' questions have on students? *Paper presented at the Annual Meeting of the American Educational Research Association, New Orleans.*

Hyman, R. T. (1987). Discussion strategies and tactics. In W. W. Wilen (Ed.) *Questions, questioning techniques, and effective teaching.* Washington, D.C.: National Education Association.

Johnson, N. L. (1992). *Thinking is the key: Questioning makes the difference.* Beavercreek, OH: Pieces of Learning.

Joy, F. (1994). *Shortcuts for teaching language usage.* Carthage, IL: Good Apple.

Kincher, J. (1990). *Psychology for kids: 40 fun tests that help you learn about yourself.* Minneapolis: Free Spirit.

Kinsman, B. (1983). *Menu madness.* Springfield, MA: Milton Bradley, Co.

Moore, G. B., & Serby, T. (1988). *Becoming whole: Learning through games.* Atlanta: TEE GEE Publishing Company.

Parker, T. (1987). *Rules of thumb.* Boston: Houghton Mifflin Company.

Riegle, R. P. (1976). Classifying classroom questions. In K. A. Strike (Ed.) *Philosophy of education 1976.* Urbana, IL: Philosophy of Education Society.

Schurr, S. (1989). *Dynamite in the classroom: A how–to handbook for teachers.* Columbus, OH: National Middle School Association.

Schurr, S. (1981). *Library lingo: Basic skills activity cards.* Nashville, TN: Incentive Publications, Inc.

Sion, C. (1985). *Recipes for tired teachers.* Reading, MA: Addison–Wesley Publishing Company, Inc.

Stock, G. (1988). *The kids' book of questions.* New York: Workman Publishing.

Villalpando, E. (1980). *Simulations.* Phoenix, AZ: Kolbe Concepts, Inc.

Weiss, D. E. (1988). *100% American.* New York: Poseidon Press.